CHILDREN OF GOD

CHILDREN

OF

GOD

Martyn Lloyd-Jones

LIFE IN CHRIST □ VOLUME THREE

STUDIES IN 1 JOHN

C R O S S W A Y   B O O K S

A DIVISION OF GOOD NEWS PUBLISHERS
WHEATON, ILLINOIS • NOTTINGHAM, ENGLAND

CREDO
PUBLISHING CORPORATION

Children of God.

First U.S. edition published 1993 by Crossway Books, a division of Good News Publishers, 1300 Crescent Street, Wheaton, Illinois 60187.

Published in association with Credo Books, P.O. Box 3175, Langley, B.C., Canada V3A 4R5.

Cover illustration: Keith Stubblefield

First printing, 1993

Printed in the United States of America

Library of Congress Cataloging-in-Publication Data
Lloyd-Jones, David Martyn.
    Life in Christ.

    Includes bibliographical references.
    Contents: v. 1. Fellowship with God — v. 2. Walking with God —
v. 3. Children of God.
    1. Bible. N. T. Epistles of John, 1st—Sermons.   2. Sermons,
English.   I. Title.
BS2805.4.L58 1993   227'.9406   92-21507
ISBN 0-89107-705-7 (v. 1)
ISBN 0-80107-777-4 (v. 3)

01	00	99	98	97	96	95	94	93
15	14	13	12	11	10	9 8	7 6	5 4	3 2 1

First British Edition 1993

ISBN 1 85684 061 1

Production and Printing in the United States of America for
CROSSWAY BOOKS
Norton Street, Nottingham, England NG7 3HR

TABLE OF CONTENTS

ACKNOWLEDGEMENTS

These sermons were first preached in Westminster Chapel. The basic editing of these sermons was carried out by Christopher Catherwood, the Doctor's eldest grandson and Editorial Director at Crossway Books in England. However, as usual, an enormous amount of work on these manuscripts has also been done by Elizabeth Catherwood, the Doctor's elder daughter and literary executrix, and to her go special thanks. (She has also done much unsung on many of his other books, so it is fitting that she should be given her due honour here.) As before, Alison Walley has not only copy edited the manuscript, but typed it onto disk for the publishers, and so full thanks are due to her as well.

Lastly, much of the vision for this series comes from the enthusiasm shown by J. I. Packer, who with his wife heard many of them preached back in the 1940's, and also to Lane Dennis, the publisher for Crossway, whose commitment to the cause of Christian truth has made their publication possible.

1

Children of God

If ye know that he is righteous, ye know that every one that doeth righteousness is born of him. Behold, what manner of love the Father hath bestowed upon us, that we should be called the sons of God: therefore the world knoweth us not, because it knew him not.

1 JOHN 2:29–3:1

In these two verses we come to a new section in this letter of the Apostle John, a section which starts at Chapter 2, verse 29. It is a new movement in the argument which John presents to the Christians to whom he was writing, and I think we may say, if such comparisons are at all possible and legitimate in such matters, that in a sense the Apostle moves here to a deeper argument, something still more profound. Let us, before we go any further, try to get the connection clear in our minds by once more standing back for a moment and looking at the general scheme, which is, I would remind you, something like this:

The Apostle's great object in writing is that these people might have a full joy; that is the theme as announced in the fourth verse of the first chapter–'these things write we unto you, that your joy may be full.' There is possible for the Christian, in this life and in this world, such as it is and with all its troubles and its trials, a fulness of joy. And the desire of this old man, as the Apostle was when he wrote his letter, is that these Christians might enjoy it to the very

9

full. So he is concerned to give them some instruction as to how that is possible, and the first big thing he tells them in this letter is that they must always bear in mind that they can have fellowship with the Father and with the Son through the Holy Spirit. Though we are here on earth, we can and do enjoy fellowship with God.

Then he goes on to show that if that is the first thing we must realise, then we must at once also realise that there are certain conditions which are absolutely vital and essential to the maintenance of that fellowship and that walk with God. And we have been considering[1] these conditions as they are outlined in the first chapter and in the whole of the second chapter down to the end of verse 28. We have taken them in detail one by one, these conditions controlling fellowship and communion with God.

They can all be summed up, in a sense, in one word, and that is the word *righteousness*. That is what John has been saying in different ways: 'God is light, and in him is no darkness at all' (1:5), therefore we must 'walk in the light' (v 7); that is to be righteous. And in the same way we must 'keep his commandments' (2:3); that is righteousness. Again, we must love the brethren; that, too, is a manifestation of righteousness. He tells us, 'Love not the world, neither the things that are in the world' (2:15); that is a negative manifestation of righteousness; and of course we must avoid all these subtle, seducing temptations to go wrong in our central belief because, apart from the Lord Jesus Christ, there is no righteousness at all.

Righteousness, then, is the thing that is essential to fellowship with God; in other words, the great stress of this epistle from beginning to end is the ethical stress. John is anxious that they see that these conditions must be observed. The great blessings come to us freely in Christ, but if we want to enjoy and to continue enjoying them, then we must walk in this righteous manner. That is the argument until the end of verse 28 of the second chapter.

But here in verse 29 we come to one of those points of transition. You see the connection; John takes it up like this: 'If ye know that he is righteous, ye know that every one that doeth righteousness is born of him.' Now that is a new key. 'In other words,' says John, 'I would have you realise that as the result of the work of the

Lord Jesus Christ you are not only in fellowship with God, you have also become children of God; you are born of God. You are not only in a new relationship in an external manner, there is a vital internal relationship. It is not merely that you are having communion and association with God, but that you are in a vital union with Him. You are in Christ, and Christ is in you, and this vital thing has happened to you.' Now that is the theme that occupies our attention in this epistle until we reach the first verse of the fourth chapter. That is the whole theme, especially of this third chapter and leading on into the fourth—the fact that we are thus born of God and in this organic, internal relationship to Him.

And here, of course, John is again producing another argument to show us the all-importance of righteousness. If righteousness is essential to an external relationship and walk with God, how much more so is it obviously essential because of the relationship that obtains between us and God in this vital organic sense. If as a companion of God I must live a righteous life, how much more so must I as a child of God live a righteous life! You see, that is why I suggest that the argument does go here to a deeper level. Comparisons, as I have suggested, are almost ridiculous at this point, because to be in communion and in fellowship with God is such a high privilege that one can regard nothing as being greater and higher. Yet we are here reminded that we are born of God, and therefore the argument for righteousness is greatly reinforced. And as we shall see, the Apostle again works out this argument of relationship to God, or being born of God, in exactly the same terms as he has worked out the argument of fellowship. We must keep the commandments; we must love the brethren; we must avoid the things of the world and those seducing spirits that would take us away from the central doctrine. It is another argument for righteous walking and living based upon this internal relationship with God, rather than on external fellowship with Him.

So that is the theme, and John announces it bluntly in his typical manner. It is the point of the twenty-ninth verse of the second chapter, and he puts it in a very interesting way. He says, 'If ye know that he is righteous, ye know [or perceive, or understand] that every one that doeth righteousness is born of him.' Now he does

not say, 'Ye know that every one that is born of him doeth righteousness'; he puts it the other way round. By which he means that
if you see men and women who are living a truly righteous life in
the sense of the New Testament term 'righteousness,' you can be
quite sure, says John, that they are born of God.

Now righteousness obviously does not just mean morality, nor
does it just mean living a good life. There are plenty of people who
are outside the Christian church today who deny the elements of
the Christian faith, but who are quite moral and decent. They are
quite good people, using the term 'good' in its moral or philosophical connotation, but they do not conform to what the New
Testament means by *righteous*. *Righteous* means the quality, the kind
of life that was lived by the Lord Jesus Christ Himself.

So John puts it like this: 'Every one that doeth righteousness . . .'
If you see people who are living the kind and quality of life that was
lived by the Lord Jesus Christ, you can know for certain, says John,
that they are born of God—they could not do it otherwise. No one
can really live the Sermon on the Mount until they are born again;
the Sermon on the Mount is impossible to the natural man or
woman. Indeed, the Christian life as a whole is impossible to them,
and it does not matter how good people are, they cannot live the
Christian life. They can live a moral, ethical life up to a point, but
they cannot live the Christian life, and the New Testament does not
even ask them to. The New Testament standard of living for the
Christian condemns the natural man or woman, and it should drive
them to see the absolute necessity of the rebirth.

Now that is John's theme in a sense, that is his great argument.
And then he takes it up like this: 'If, then, we are born of God, does
it not follow of necessity that we must be living a certain quality and
kind of life?' That is the argument that he works out from verse 3
in chapter 3 to the end of the chapter. 'It is inconsistent if we are
not,' he says; he ridicules it. He says, in effect, 'If you are breaking
the commandments and are living in sin, you cannot claim you are
a child of God. If you live that sort of life, you are not a child of
God, you are a child of the devil. The child of God must be living
a different type of life.' And he continues in the same way with the
love of the brethren and these other matters.

However, before he goes on to work out the argument which is inevitable because we are children of God, he pauses for a moment in the first three verses of chapter 3 just to contemplate what exactly it means when we are told that we are the children of God. He has mentioned being 'born of him,' but it is as if he says to himself, 'I cannot just leave it like that as a closing, passing phrase. The whole thing is so wonderful and amazing that we must stop for a moment to worship and adore as we realise what we are talking about. Before I work out the argument, let me remind you again of what you are and who you are.'

Now those who are interested in what we may describe as the mechanics of Scripture, or the form of the composition as distinct from the message, will recall that this is very typical of John. Do you remember how we had to pause halfway through the second chapter and look together at verses 12, 13 and 14 where John said, 'I write unto you, little children, because your sins are forgiven you. . . .' You remember how we pointed out that he interrupted his argument in order to remind them who and what they were, and then he made his argument inevitable. And he is doing the same thing again here; so this is, as it were, the pause: 'Behold, what manner of love the Father hath bestowed upon us, that we should be called the sons [or children] of God: therefore the world knoweth us not, because it knew him not. Beloved, now are we the sons of God, and it doth not yet appear what we shall be: but we know that, when he shall appear, we shall be like him; for we shall see him as he is. And every man that hath this hope in him purifieth himself, even as he is pure.' And then he goes on with the argument, but before he does so, he asks us to pause for a little to contemplate this amazing, wonderful thing that is true of us as Christian people. And now I want us to look at it only in terms of the first verse; the three verses are perhaps the three most moving verses in the entire epistle, and they do merit our detailed consideration.

Before we go on to do this, we must just refer to the fact that in the Revised and other versions there is an additional phrase in verse 1: 'Behold, what manner of love the Father hath bestowed upon us, that we should be called the sons of God *and such we are*. . . .' This phrase is to be found in some of the best manuscripts, and probably, therefore, it was in the original document. It is not, of course, a material point, because he says the same thing in verse 2: 'Beloved, now are we the sons of God'; so it is, therefore, just a matter of interest from the standpoint of textual criticism. So now, having dealt with that, let us look at this first verse. First of all, let us look for a moment at what we are, we who are Christians. According to John, we are 'the sons of God,' or, better perhaps, 'the children of God.' What does this mean exactly? Well, we can analyse it, I think, quite simply and legitimately by putting it like this: As children we stand in a certain position; a child is in a certain relationship to the parents—it has a certain station and is therefore entitled to certain privileges. The word *child* or *son*, especially at this point, carries with it a kind of legal statement which defines the relationship and position and status. A child is one who is related to a given parent in a way that no one else is; so you can look at it in that external manner, from the pure standpoint of legal relationship.

And here John asks us to pause and contemplate this wonderful thing, that you and I, such as we are, here in this world of time, are in that position, in that relationship to God. We are 'children of God'; we stand in this unique and separate relationship to Him. 'But surely,' says someone, 'are not all people children of God? Don't you believe in the universal Fatherhood of God and the universal brotherhood of man; isn't that something which is taught in Scripture?' The reply is, of course, that there is a sense in which all men and women are children of God, in the sense of being the offspring of God; by which we mean that they have been created by God and derived from Him. But at the same time, Scripture is very careful to differentiate that from those who come into this special relationship of sonship to God as the result of the work of the Lord Jesus Christ.

John is going on in this chapter to differentiate between the children of God and the children of the devil, and our Lord Himself did the same, as we read in John's Gospel where He turned to certain people and said, 'Ye are of your father the devil.' You are not the children of God, he tells them, you are the children of the devil, and 'the lusts of your father ye will do' (John 8:44). So that this idea of the universal Fatherhood of God and the universal brotherhood of man is not a Scriptural statement at all. Indeed it violates, if we stop at it, that which is the plain and clear teaching of the New Testament. It is only those who are born again, who are in Christ and who are truly the children of God, who have 'the Spirit of adoption' and cry out, 'Abba, Father' (Rom 8:15); it is they who are in this intimate relationship to God. The other is something that belongs to creation, not to the realm of salvation, and the Bible says that those who are not in this new relationship are outside the life of God. 'This is life eternal,' says Jesus Christ, 'that they might know thee, the only true God, and Jesus Christ, whom thou hast sent' (John 17:3). Apart from that, we are outside the life of God; we remain dead in trespasses and sins and have none of the privileges of sonship. 'But,' says John, 'we are called the children of God,' and 'called' does not merely mean an external application or appellation—it means that we are, we have become, the children of God.

But it does not only mean that, of course; it means also that we share the very nature of God, and that is why the authorities are all careful to point out that the right translation here is 'children of God' and not 'sons of God.' Is there a difference between a child and a son? Well, there is in this sense, that the word *son* emphasises a legal, external relationship, whereas the word *child* always puts the emphasis upon the common nature, that the child is derived from the parent and shares the nature and the blood of the parent. It emphasises this internal, vital, organic aspect of the relationship rather than the legal position. And what John, therefore, is reminding us of here is that we who are truly Christians are sharers of the very life of God.

Peter expresses this by saying that we have become 'partakers of the divine nature' (2 Pet 1:4). It is difficult to put this into words, and yet it is something that is taught everywhere in the New Testament. The figure of the vine and the branches in John 15 puts it perfectly; the branch is in the vine, and so the life of the vine, the sap, the vitality passes into the branches—there is that organic relationship; and that is what John is emphasising here, so that we share the nature of God.

Or we can put it like this: As children we are members of the family of God. The Apostle Paul makes that point in writing to the

Ephesians, where he tells them, 'At one time ye were without Christ, being aliens from the commonwealth of Israel.' But 'now,' he goes on, they have been made 'fellow citizens with the saints, and of the household of God' (Eph 2:12, 19). We have become members of God's family; we really are in that relationship to Him because we have His nature. Because we have received of His life, we, as children, belong to His family, we belong to his household, and we are therefore in this unique relationship to Him. And that, of course, in turn means that we are heirs of God; as Paul says in Romans 8:17: 'If children, then heirs; heirs of God, and joint-heirs with Christ.'

Now these are some of the things that are immediately conjured up as we just ask the question raised by the first verse—What are we? The answer is that we are 'called the children of God,' and there is a sense in which this is so staggering and so overwhelming that we find it almost impossible to accept it, and to retain the idea in our minds. Yet that is what is said about Christians everywhere in the New Testament. Let us never again think of the Christian as just someone who is trying to live a good life, trying to be a little bit better than somebody else, a person with a belief in doing certain things, going through certain forms and ceremonials and keeping certain regulations dictated by the church. Christians do all that, but before all that is this vital fact that they are children of God. They have been born again, born from above, born of the Spirit; they have received something of the very nature and life of God Himself. They are transformed people, they are a new creation, and they are thus absolutely, essentially different from those who have not experienced that. That is the very basic thing which the New Testament everywhere emphasises concerning the Christian.

Then the second question is, How have we become this—how have we become children of God? John answers that in this way: 'Behold, what manner of love the Father hath bestowed upon us.' This is a very interesting way of putting it. John does not merely say that God has shown His love to us, nor that He has revealed it or manifested it or indicated it. He does not merely say that God loves us, though He does love us and He has shown and displayed His love to us. 'Yes,' says John, 'but He has gone further—He has *bestowed* His love upon us.' Now that means there is a sense in which God has put His love into us, implanted Himself if you like, infused or injected His love within us, and we must emphasise that, because what really matters is the word *that*, which should be translated *in order that*. 'Behold, what manner of love the Father hath bestowed upon us in order that we may become, be made, the children of God'; that is what John actually says.

In other words, what really makes us children of God is that God has put His own life into us. God's nature is love, and he has put His nature into us so that we have the love of God. We cannot be children of God if we are not like God; the child is like the parent, the offspring proclaims the parentage, and God in that way makes us His children. He puts His own nature into us, and we become His children, and that nature which is in God is in us, and it is acting and manifesting and expressing itself. Paul says that 'the love of God is shed abroad in our hearts by the Holy Ghost' (Rom 5:5). Here again, I say, is something that is so wonderful and surpassingly strange that it is almost impossible for us to receive and to hold on to it, and yet nothing less than that is true of the Christian. John will make use of this argument later on in this chapter, where he says that if you have the love of God in you, you are bound to love one another. Even though your brother may be unworthy, you must love him. Is that not the whole message of Christ's death upon the cross? He is in you, and He has made you children of God.

Let us now look at the third aspect of this matter; let me emphasise the mystery of all this. '. . . therefore the world knoweth us not, because it knew him not.' This is a mystery. This condition in which we find ourselves as Christians, this being a child of God, is a great mystery. The world does not understand it; it does not know what we are talking about. The world ridicules it 'because it knew him not'; the world does not understand this sort of thing; it says, 'You Christians claim that you are children of God, that something of the divine nature is in you and that you are different, separated from other people. Away with your suggestion!' Says the world, 'Do you mean that you people, as I see you to be, are children of God, shar-

ers and partakers of His divine nature? No; you are just ordinary
people like everybody else.'

'It is all right,' says John; 'don't be upset if the world says that
to you—"it knew him not." The world said, "This fellow, this son
of Joseph and Mary, this carpenter of Galilee, that talks and says,
'I and the Father are one,' who is He?"' The world did not know
Him; it saw nothing else; it did not see the Godhead; it did not see
the Trinity that was there, and it does not see it in you,' says John.
'So don't be surprised if you are misunderstood or if you are
laughed at. The world may say that you have religious mania and
count you soft or say that you have suddenly developed a psychological complex, but don't be surprised,' continues John. 'It did not
know Him, and it won't know you. This thing of which I am speaking is only discerned spiritually. It is something hidden, something
within, in exactly the same way as the Godhead was veiled by the
flesh of Christ, hidden and revealed at the same time—and so it is
true of the Christian; we have the divine nature within us, and yet
it is veiled, and the world does not see through that. But it is all
right,' says John; 'this is a mystery, this is something internal.'

You will find exactly the same idea in Revelation 2:17 where we
are told that a secret name is given to Christians, to the children of
God who receive a sign and a name, and no one understands this
hidden name but the Christians themselves; that is the same idea
exactly. It is a great mystery; in a sense it is one of the most glorious aspects of the Christian life. The world does not know us, but
we know Christ, and we know one another, and that is proof of life.
We are aware that something is happening to us; we are aware that
God has dealt with us and has done something to us; we know that
we are new creatures. We are aware that we cannot explain ourselves to ourselves except in terms of Christ, and we know when
we see it in another; nobody else does, but we know one another.

This is one of the most mysterious aspects of Christian life and
experience. Those who have the life of God always know one
another, and they feel an affinity and an attraction which no one
else can understand. Other people may mix with them, they may
know people very well, and yet there is something those others
have not got. There is a barrier; ours is a life which does not show

itself in external affairs, it does not show itself even in the mode and manner of living, but it is a life which recognises itself in the other, and this is a great mystery. But it is a great reality at the same time. 'The world knoweth us not'; it does not understand us; it says, 'What have you people got—what is this something you are always speaking about?' It looks on from the outside but cannot discern it. If you want a perfect commentary on what I am trying to say, read 1 Corinthians 2, especially towards the end: 'He that is spiritual judgeth all things, yet he himself is judged of no man' (1 Cor 2:15). That is it; we know one another, but no one else knows. We understand, they do not, and 'the world knoweth us not, because it knew him not'; this is the mystery of this gift of life and of the life that is within us.

But lastly, there is the marvel of it all. 'Behold, what manner of love'! Words, of course, become meaningless at this point; there is nothing to do but to gaze upon it and to wonder at it all, to stand in amazement and in astonishment. Oh, the quality of this love! Just realise what it means, the freeness of it all, that you and I should be called and become children of God! The freeness of this love that has looked upon us in spite of our sin, in spite of our recalcitrance, in spite of our unworthiness, in spite of our foulness as a result of the Fall and our own actions. Oh, the love that has not merely forgiven us but has given itself to us, that has entered into us and shared its own nature with us; stand in awe at the greatness of it all! Think of what it cost Him, our Lord Jesus Christ, to come into the world, to live in the world, suffering its treatment, staggering up Golgotha with that cross upon His shoulders and being nailed to the tree. Think of Him dying, suffering the agony and the shame of it all in order that you and I might become children of God.

'Behold, what manner of love'—you cannot understand it, you cannot explain it. The only thing we can say is that it is the eternal love, it is the love of God and is self-generated, produced by nothing but itself, so that in spite of us and all that is true of us He came and died and suffered so much. The Son of God became the Son of Man that we, the sons of men, might become the children of God. It is true, we are that; we have been made that. Amazing, incredible, yet true!

2

Destined for Glory

Beloved, now are we the sons of God, and it doth not yet
appear what we shall be: but we know that, when he shall
appear, we shall be like him; for we shall see him as he is.

1 JOHN 3:2

I suppose we must agree that nothing more sublime than this has
ever been written, and any man who has to preach upon such
a text or upon such a word must be unusually conscious of his
own smallness and inadequacy and unworthiness. One's tendency
with a statement like this always is just to stand in wonder and
amazement at it. I have never chosen, in and of myself, to preach
upon this text. I have often felt that I would like to, but there are
certain great words like this in Scripture of which frankly I am, in
a sense, frightened; frightened as a preacher, lest anything that I say
may detract from them or may rob anyone of their greatness and
their glory. That may be wrong, but this is how it always affects me.

However, here we are, working through this first epistle of John
and we come to this magnificent and glorious statement. So we
must look at it, for it is to do violence to Scripture not to consider
and examine it, and we must not be content with some mere general effect as we read these words. They are moving, and yet we
must not let ourselves merely be moved in an emotional, and still
less in a sentimental, sense; so it behooves us to examine the statement and to see something of its richness and its wonder.

Furthermore, it is when one confronts a text like this that one realises what a privilege it is to be a Christian minister. I am rather sorry for anyone who has not had to spend a week with a verse like this! I assure you it is a very enriching experience, a humbling one and an uplifting one. There is nothing surely in life that can be more wonderful or more glorious than to have to spend a week or so with a word like this, looking at it, listening to it, and considering what others have said about it. It is indeed something for which one humbly thanks God.

What we have here is one of those great New Testament descriptions of the Christian and of the Christian's life in this world. A number of things inevitably must strike us on the very surface before we come to any detailed analysis. The first thing is how utterly inadequate are our ordinary, customary ideas of ourselves as Christian people. When you read this, and then when you think of yourself and what you generally see and observe about yourself and about your life as a Christian in this world, oh, how inadequate are all our ideas! Or take it as it was put in that hymn of the great Richard Baxter:

> Lord, it belongs not to my care
>   Whether I die or live;
> To love and serve Thee is my share,
>   And this Thy grace must give.
>
> If life be long, I will be glad
>   That I may long obey;
> If short, yet why should I be sad
>   To soar to endless day?
>
> Christ leads me through no darker rooms
>   Than He went through before;
> He that into God's kingdom comes
>   Must enter by this door.
>
> Come, Lord, when grace hath made me meet
>   Thy blessed face to see;

For if Thy work on earth be sweet,
What will Thy glory be?

Then shall I end my sad complaints
And weary sinful days,
And join with the triumphant saints
Who sing Jehovah's praise.

My knowledge of that life is small;
The eye of faith is dim:
But 'tis enough that Christ knows all,
And I shall be with Him.

Can we really say those words from the heart? Is that our view of ourselves and of our life as Christian people in this world? Is that our view of the possibility of our life being short or of being long? Is that our view of life and of death and of eternity? Well, according to this text we are looking at in this chapter, that is the Christian view. 'Beloved, now are we the sons of God, and it doth not yet appear what we shall be; but we know that, when he shall appear, we shall be like him; for we shall see him as he is.'

I do feel that this is perhaps the greatest weakness of all in the Christian church, that we fail to realise what we are, or who we are. We spend our time in arguing about the implications of the Christian truth or the application of this, that and the other. But the central thing is to realise what the Christian *is*. We grumble and complain, and it is all due to the fact that we have not really seen ourselves in terms of this picture. Surely, as we read these words, we must of necessity be humbled, indeed in a sense humiliated, as we realise the inadequacy of our ideas and the unworthiness of our view of ourselves as Christian people.

Or let me put it to you like this: is it not the honest truth that most of the unhappiness that we experience in this life is due to our failure to realise this truth? We are full of complaints and unhappiness. They arise partly from our own faults, partly from what others do to us or from what the world as a whole does to us. But all our unhappiness is ultimately to be traced back to this, that we are looking at the things that are happening to us, instead of looking at this vision that is held there before us. It is because we do not see ourselves as the children of God and going through this life and world in the way that this text indicates; that is why our unhappiness tends to get us down. We do not relate it to the whole; we do not put it in its context; we live too much with the things that are immediately in front of us instead of putting everything into the context of our standing and of our destiny.

In the same way we must at once realise, I think, that most of our failure to live the Christian life as we should live it is also due to the same cause. If only we realised who we are, then the problem of conduct would almost automatically be solved. This is how parents often deal with this problem in instructing their children. They say to them, 'Now remember who you are.' In other words it is our failure to realise who we are that causes us to stumble on this whole question of moral conduct and behaviour. This objection to the stringent demands of the gospel is due to one thing only, namely that we do not realise who we are. If once we saw ourselves as we are depicted here, there would be no need to persuade us to live the Christian life. As the next verse tells us, we would feel that we have to, it is inevitable, it is logical. The whole trouble is to be traced to a failure to realise our true greatness and position and standing.

In other words, the more I read the New Testament, the more I am impressed by the fact that every appeal for conduct and good living and behaviour is always made in terms of our *position*. The Bible never asks us to do anything without reminding us first of all who we are; you always get doctrine before practical exhortation. Look at any epistle you like and you will always find it; these men, under the inspiration of the Holy Spirit, first of all tell us, 'This is what you are as the result of the work of Christ—therefore . . .' It is never the other way round. To put it bluntly, the New Testament is not interested in the conduct of people who are not Christians. It has nothing to tell them except that they are destined for hell and for perdition. That is its only statement. They must repent, and until they repent and believe on the Lord Jesus Christ it is not interested in their behaviour—that is its one message to them. But the moment they become Christians, it is vitally interested in their conduct; it appeals to them because of what has happened.

Or we can put it like this: there is no comfort or encouragement offered in the Bible to anybody except those who are the children of God. When things go wrong in the world, people tend to turn to religion. In times of difficulty there is always a sort of turning to God; people pray to Him and think of the gospel. But in the first instance, the one message of the gospel to them is still the message of condemnation; it warns them to flee from the wrath to come. The gospel is not some psychological agency just to tide people over little troubles, nor is it meant to make us feel happy for the moment. No, this consolation and comfort which is absolute and eternal is always solidly based upon our understanding and realisation of who we are and what we are. The key to the understanding of everything in the New Testament is that we should realise what Christ has done for us and what we are in Him as the result of His work.

Now that is the very thing that John is concerned about in this epistle. His appeal at this point is based upon what we are. We have seen that John is out to comfort these people, and he shows them that it is vitally important, if they are really to reap the full benefits of the Christian gospel, that they should be living the Christian life. This is a great appeal for righteousness, keeping the commandments of God, loving the brethren, hating the world. Someone says, 'Why should I do these things?' John replies, 'Beloved, realise what you are and who you are, and if you do, you will see that these things follow automatically.' That is what he does in this second verse; so let us look at it together.

The first thing we must do with this word is to be careful we do not misinterpret it. The very form of the words which are to be found, especially in the Authorised Version, almost tend to make us misinterpret or misunderstand them. There is a kind of suggested contrast in the text which in reality is not there at all. The danger as you read this statement is that you will contrast the 'now' and 'not yet appear what we shall be.' Furthermore this word 'but' which you find in various versions is not in the best manuscripts, and it should not be there.

So there is no contrast between 'now' and 'shall be,' and this word 'but' should be omitted—all these statements are positive. We must never read this verse in such a way as to regard it as a kind of alternating series of certainties and uncertainties. They are all a series of positive statements; the Apostle in each case is telling us what he does know. Also this word 'appear' which is used is not the best translation; it ought to be 'manifested,' so that we read our text like this: 'Beloved, now are we the sons [or, better, children] of God, and what we shall be has not yet been manifested; we know that when he shall appear, we shall be like him, for we shall see him as he is.' We are the children of God; we know what we are going to be, but it has not been manifested; we know that when He shall be manifested Himself, we shall be like Him, for we shall see Him as He is.

In other words, the text is a great series of positive statements. John says, in effect, 'Here we are—Christian people in this world, and the world does not understand us. It may perhaps hate us; it may be unkind and cruel to us. Very well,' says John, 'don't be disturbed or upset by that; don't think of yourselves or estimate yourselves in terms of what the world says about Christians because the world can know nothing at all about it. It did not know Christ when He came; it has never known God; so the world, when it laughs at you, is giving you a great confirmation of your faith.'

The Bible is very fond of saying something like that; it suggests that we are in a very bad condition if all men speak well of us. 'Yea,' says Paul to Timothy, 'and all that will live godly in Christ Jesus shall suffer persecution' (2 Tim 3:12); we ought rather to be concerned about ourselves if the world thinks highly of us and seems to think it does understand us. No, the world knows us not because it knew Him not. 'The one thing that matters,' says John, 'is that you should know yourself, that you should know what you are as a Christian, that you should know these things and that you should know Him.'

Let me, therefore, divide up the verse like this: There are three main statements made here by the Apostle. The first is that we know that we are the children of God. The second is that we know we are destined for glory. And the third thing we know is something concerning that glory. Those are the three positive statements in the verse.

The first thing, then, is that we know that we are the children of God. 'Beloved, now are we the sons of God.' You notice that he does not say, 'we shall be,' but rather 'we are.' We have already dealt with this in a sense in dealing with the first verse. I am just emphasising it once more. The Christian is meant to know exactly where he is and where he stands. He is not left groping in the dark, neither is he just meant to be hoping. The Christian is someone who should be able to say, 'I know, I am persuaded, I am certain.' These things are facts.

Let me put it strongly like this: we shall never be more the children of God than we are now. I do not hesitate to make that statement. I am as certainly a child of God now as I shall be in glory; I shall be a much better man then, but I shall be no more a child of God. The human analogy puts that perfectly; conduct does not determine relationship; relationship is something vital, organic, internal. The prodigal son was as much the son of his father as was the elder brother. Behaviour, conduct and appearance—all these things do not determine relationship, thank God! Therefore we are children of God now as much as we shall be throughout the countless ages of eternity in glory. You are either a child of God or you are not, and once you are a child of God you are His child for ever and ever in that divine and eternal relationship. You cannot be a Christian one day and not the next day. Once you are born of the Spirit and born of God, you are a child of God. You may vary a lot in your conduct and behaviour, but we must never hold the view of holiness or backsliding or any one of these doctrines which gives the impression you can be in and out of the relationship. You cannot! Relationship is something that is fixed and remains. Other things are variable and come and go, but, 'Beloved, now are we the sons of God.' So again I ask the question, do we know this, are we quite certain about it? I am not asking at the moment, 'How do you live?' I am not asking you your views on various matters. No, my question is, do you know you are a child of God?

But how does one know this—how is this knowledge obtainable and possible? What indications do I have that I am a child of God?

Well, here are just some of the answers. Men and women who are children of God are aware of a new life, a new nature within them. They can say, 'I live; yet not I' (Gal 2:20). They are aware that there is another factor, another person, another presence. In a real sense, in a true sense, they are aware of a kind of dualism—they themselves, and yet somebody else. And they can only explain themselves to themselves in terms of this other life and this other person—I, yet not I, but Christ. One like that is aware of a new nature, another life, a different order of being from that which is merely natural.

Or let me put it like this: we know that we are children of God when we are deeply aware of sin within. I emphasise that deliberately. It is only the children of God who realise that they have a sinful nature. The unregenerate, the natural men and women, are not aware of a sinful nature. They may admit that they do certain things which they should not do, but begin to tell them that they have a sinful nature, that they are dead in trespasses and sins, and they will hate you and begin to defend themselves; they hate preaching that condemns them.

No, it is only the children of God who realise that they have an utterly sinful nature. It is only a saint like Charles Wesley who says, 'Vile and full of sin I am.' It was Saint Paul who said, 'For I know that in me (that is, in my flesh), dwelleth no good thing' (Rom 7:18). It is the Christian who cries out and says, 'O wretched man that I am! who shall deliver me from the body of this death?' (Rom 7:24). An unregenerate believer has never uttered such words and never can—it is impossible. It is the indwelling of the Holy Spirit that exposes our sinful nature and the depths of sin and iniquity that reside in our hearts. 'The heart is deceitful above all things, and desperately wicked: who can know it?' says Jeremiah (Jer 17:9). 'I dare not trust my sweetest frame,' says the hymn-writer. All these things are indications of the new nature—an awareness of sin and above all a desire to be rid of it. If you are hating the sin within you and longing to be delivered and emancipated from it, I assure you, you are a child of God—it is one of the best signs.

Next there is a desire for God and a desire for the things of God and a desire to walk in the ways of God. Do you know what it is to long to know God better, to long to know Him truly? Do you feel that you wish you really could say those words of Richard Baxter from the depth of your being? Have you felt that you are a child of God? Have you wished that you could say this? Well, I can honestly tell you, that is never an unregenerate person's desire. His mind is enmity against God; he wants certain blessings from God when it suits him. The people who delight in the things of God and like to read the Bible and want to pray and are grieved that they do not pray more—all these are indications of being children of God.

Then there is what the Apostle Paul calls 'the Spirit of adoption, whereby we cry, Abba, Father' (Rom 8:15), the feeling that God is not just some great potentate far away in some distant eternity, but that somehow or another we do know that He loves us. We are aware of a filial feeling with respect to Him, and there is something within us that cries out, 'Father!' We are aware that God is coming nearer to us and that we are related to Him.

And then there is one other thing which I have already mentioned, the love of the brethren. I say again, a very good and a very subtle test of whether we are children of God is whether we really love and like God's people and whether we like to be amongst them. Do not misunderstand me—that does not mean that there are not certain things in Christian people which you may find objectionable! But do you feel instinctively drawn to a good person? Do you feel an affinity with people who like to talk about these things, and with those who are the children of God? Or are you still fascinated by the glamour of the world? Which do you *really* like; which do you prefer? The children of God love to realise that they are in the family; they love the brethren; they feel, 'These are my people— these are the people with whom I want to spend eternity.'

These are just some of the tests which we apply to ourselves to prove whether we are indeed the children of God.

Now let us go on to the second principle, which is that we know that we are destined for glory. 'Beloved, now are we the sons of God, and it doth not yet appear what we shall be.' What we are going to be has not yet been revealed to us, but we know that we are destined for it. That is obviously what John means. He is not here in a sort of uncertain state which says, 'Well, we are the children of God. At the present time I do not quite know what is going to happen to us, but no doubt it is going to be all right.' Not at all! John has seen something of the glory, and he says, it has not yet been revealed to this world which does not understand it, but it will be revealed.

We can put it like this: Here we are in a state of humiliation, but we are going to be in a state of glorification. Do you not see that as Christian people we, in a sense, have to retrace the steps trodden before us by our Lord? You remember how Richard Baxter puts that—we have to enter into the room which He has already been through here on earth in a state of humiliation—born in Bethlehem, working as a carpenter, people not recognising Him—it was humiliation. While He was on the earth that was His condition, and the world did not know Him. 'He came unto his own, and his own received him not' (John 1:11); the world, His own world, rejected Him; His own people rejected Him. Yes, but He is no longer in the state of humiliation; He has passed on to glory, and He is in a state of glorification. The Apostle Paul had a vision of Him there on the road to Damascus; John had a vision on the island of Patmos; there He is in glory, and you and I are to retrace those very steps. Here we are in a state of humiliation, yes, but as certainly as He has gone before, we also shall go on to glory.

'Let not your heart be troubled,' said our Lord, 'ye believe in God, believe also in me. In my Father's house are many mansions: if it were not so, I would have told you. I go to prepare a place for you. And if I go and prepare a place for you, I will come again, and receive you unto myself' (John 14:1-2). That is it! It is the same thing exactly.

Christians, therefore, know that they are destined for that state of glory; it is part of their essential belief. It is as much a part of their belief as their forgiveness of sins by the work of Christ upon the cross. So what the Christian says is, 'I am destined for glory. It has not come yet, but it is coming, and I am going on to it.' It will be manifested for certain, and so they are full of confidence and assurance. Paul in that great eighth chapter of the epistle to the Romans is in reality saying the same thing. This verse is John's way of saying, 'For I am persuaded that neither death, nor life, nor angels, nor principalities, nor powers, nor things present, nor things to come, nor height, nor depth, nor any other creature, shall be able to separate us from the love of God, which is in Christ Jesus our Lord' (Rom 8:38-39). Your glorification and mine is an absolute certainty. As certainly as our Lord has entered into His glory, you and I who are children of God shall enter into it also.

It does not look like it now—John agrees entirely—it 'doth not yet appear,' and the world is against us—it does not understand it. That is exactly how it was with Him, but the thing is certain.

On what grounds can I be sure of this? Here is my answer: the purposes of God. Consider Paul again: 'For whom he did foreknow, he also did predestinate to be conformed to the image of his Son, that he [Christ] might be the firstborn among many brethren' (Rom 8:29). That is a perfect statement of the whole thing. Your glorification and mine is a part of the purpose of God in salvation, and when God has purposed and planned a thing, it is certain and nothing can prevent it. Read again that mighty logic of Romans 8 and you will see it put perfectly. I can therefore rest my confidence of glorification upon the promises of God, and the promises of God are based upon the character of God. God cannot, because He is God, break His promises, and He has also given an oath, so we have a double assurance. The promises are there with His purposes and His character at the back of them.

If you are still uncertain, add the power of God. 'For thy sake we are killed all the day long; we are accounted as sheep for the slaughter,' but what does it matter? 'In all these things we are more than conquerors through him that loved us' (Rom 8:36-37). 'Who shall separate us from the love of Christ?' (Rom 8:35). It is impossible; there is nothing that can do so. We talk about the power of God, the One who made the world and the One who could end it in a second. All the almighty, illimitable and absolute power of God guarantees my glorification.

Indeed, I have an even further argument than that. What we are now is a guarantee, in a sense, of what we are going to be. Our sonship is in itself a guarantee of our glorification because God never starts a work and then gives it up. 'He which hath begun a good work in you will perform it until the day of Jesus Christ'

(Phil 1:6). You and I start things and drop them; that is typical of mankind as a result of sin. But whatever God begins, God continues, and God will end it in absolute perfection. If therefore I am but a child, insignificant, unworthy, immature, the fact that I am alive is proof that I am going on to ultimate maturity; Christ is 'the first-born among many brethren,' and He is preparing and leading others, a great crowd of brethren, until eventually we arrive in eternal glory. Do you know that you are destined for glory, my friend; do you know within yourself that that is something that is awaiting you, that you are being led and taken on to that glory which awaits you? John says, 'We *know*' this.

But that brings me to my last point. What do we know concerning this glory? These are the things that are indicated. We know that this glory is to be ushered in by the appearing, or the manifestation, of the Lord Jesus Christ Himself. 'We know that, when he shall appear, we shall be like him.' This is the great New Testament doctrine of the Second Coming, but God forbid that we should immediately begin to think of our several theories of this, that, or the other, of how it is going to happen. All I know is this, that the Lord Jesus Christ will come again. Let us take the Scripture in its broad statement, and let us beware of robbing ourselves, I say, of the life-giving glorious doctrine by thus particularising these mere theories and philosophies rather than accepting this true exposition of Scripture.

The Second Coming is a fact. The Lord Jesus Christ is coming again, and there will be a judgment, and all that is sinful and evil will be consigned to the lake of fire and destroyed throughout all eternity; and there is to be 'new heavens and a new earth, wherein dwelleth righteousness' (2 Pet 3:13). When He comes, these things will take place; that is the way the glory will be ushered in. The world is to be rid of everything that is impure, foul and unworthy; 'the elements shall melt with fervent heat' (2 Pet 3:10); there is to be a renovation and a regeneration; there will be a new world, and all evil will be banished. That is how the glory is to be ushered in, and I know that whatever the appearances may be in this world, as certainly as the Lord Jesus Christ came into the world the first time as a babe in Bethlehem, He will come again as the King of kings and Lord of lords, and He will wind up the affairs of this universe of time. I know that it is certain.

Furthermore, 'we shall see him as he is.' 'Now we see through a glass, darkly, but then face to face: now I know in part; but then shall I know even as also I am known' (1 Cor 13:12). Do you know that you are destined for that? We shall see Him as He is—blessed, glorious vision to see the Son of God in all His glory, as He is, face to face—you standing and looking at Him and enjoying Him for all eternity. It is only then that we will begin to understand what He did for us, the price He paid, the cost of our salvation. Oh, let us hold on to this! Shame on us for ever grumbling or complaining; shame on us for ever saying that the lot of the Christian is hard; shame on us for ever objecting to the demands of this glorious gospel; shame on us for ever half-heartedly worshipping, praising and loving His honour and His glory. You and I are destined for that vision glorious; we shall see Him as He is, face to face.

But consider something still more amazing and incredible. We shall be like Him. 'We know that, when he shall appear, we shall be like him; for we shall see him as he is.' This is John's way of putting the whole doctrine of the resurrection of our very bodies, the ultimate final resurrection, the ultimate glorification of God's people. What John is telling us, in other words, is that when that great day comes we shall not only see Him, we shall be made like Him. Paul says that God's purpose is that we shall be 'conformed to the image of his Son' (Rom 8:29). That is the argument, and that is the doctrine.

In other words, while we are here on earth, the Holy Spirit is working in us, doing His work of holiness in us and ridding us of sin so that eventually we shall be faultless, blameless, without spot and without rebuke. We shall have been delivered from every sin and vestige and appearance of sin within us, and in addition to that, our very bodies shall be changed and shall be glorified. Paul says that we expect Christ to come from heaven for this reason—that He shall change the body of our humiliation 'that it may be fashioned like unto his glorious body' (Phil 3:21). There will be an amazing change then in those who love Him when He appears. Again, read 1 Corinthians 15 where Paul tells us that 'we shall all be changed,

in a moment' (vv 51-52). Our bodies will be glorified; there will be
something of the radiance of His own glory in your body and mine,
so that in this new heaven and new earth we shall have bodies made
fit for our glorified spirits. We shall be like Him.

The New Testament does not tell us much more than that,
because we could not stand it; our language is inadequate, and if it
were adequate, the description would be so baffling we could not
tolerate it, the thing is so glorious and wonderful. When the three
disciples were with our Lord on the Mount of Transfiguration, they
could not stand it; the magnificence of the glory, the brightness of
the appearance was too great. Consider too what happened to Paul
when he had one glimpse of that vision on the road to Damascus—
he was blinded. No, I could not stand it as I am as the result of sin;
but when I am delivered from sin and the bondage of corruption,
and when I have a new, glorified body, I will be able to stand it. I
will look at Him, I will see Him face to face, I will see Him as He
is, I will be like Him. If I were not like Him I could not stand it—
that is John's argument.

I believe there is another thing here, and that is that as we look
at Him, we become like Him; and as we continually look at Him,
we shall be perfected.

> *Changed from glory into glory*
> *Till in heaven we take our place*
> *Till we cast our crowns before Him,*
> *Lost in wonder, love and praise.*

> Charles Wesley

We are changed into this same image, from glory into glory, as
we look at Him and contemplate Him; and when we see Him perfectly, it will be an absolute change.

Those, then, are some of the things of which the Christian is
sure, according to the Apostle John. We know that we are the children of God, we know that we are destined for glory, and we know
that glory is to be ushered in by His manifestation. We know that
then we shall see Him as He is, and, wonder of wonders, we shall

be like Him! What blessed vision, what glorious hope, that I, small, insignificant, fallible, sinful, unworthy, shall be like Him, 'the first-born among many brethren,' and made conformable to His glorious nature. Beloved people, let us lay hold on this hope and look upon it and meditate upon it day by day.

3

Holiness

And every man that hath this hope in him purifieth himself,
even as he is pure.

1 JOHN 3:3

This verse, as the very first word 'and' reminds us, is one that
is intimately connected with the previous verse. Now these
two verses in their relationship to one another remind me
very forcibly of those incidents in the life and ministry of our Lord
which we find recorded in the Gospels, in which we have two
scenes, the one immediately following the other. The first is the
scene on the Mount of Transfiguration where our Lord went up
onto the Mount with Peter and James and John and was transfig-
ured before them. Then, after the amazing and extraordinary
things that happened there, they went down again onto the plain,
where they were confronted by the case of that poor lunatic boy
who had been brought by his father to the disciples in order that
they might heal him. It is a familiar and well-known contrast
between the glory and the wonder of the Transfiguration and the
heavenly scene upon the Mount, and the scene of the problem and
the unhappiness and the misery which was found down on the
plain; and the interesting thing, of course, about the two incidents
is how the one immediately follows upon the other (Luke 9:28-43).

And there is a sense in which one is constrained to remember
those two incidents as one reads these two verses. We have been on

the mountain of God, and we were shown things unseen. We were
given that glimpse of glory, of the glory that awaits us and the
astounding and amazing things to which we are heirs. But here we
are now, as it were, back to earth again. We are reminded that
before we enter into that glory and enjoy it in all its fulness, certain
things remain and abound. We are still men and women in the flesh,
in this world which, John has already told us, does not know us. It
does not understand us and, indeed, it is opposed to us and inimi-
cal to our highest and best interests. Yet though we do feel that, we
must be very careful—and that is the point I want to emphasise most
of all here—we must be very careful lest we regard this third verse
as some sort of anticlimax after the second. It is not an anticlimax,
and to regard it as such is simply a manifestation of our sinful
nature.

Indeed, not only is this verse not an anticlimax, it is not even a
contrast to the second verse; the very word *and* which connects the
two verses reminds us that these two things are indissolubly bound
together and that verse 3 follows verse 2 very directly and immediately and, indeed, of necessity. There is a sense in which we can
say that the whole object of verse 2 is to lead to verse 3, and if we
fail to regard the second verse in that light, if we fail to see that its
real object and purpose is to prepare the way for this third verse,
then we have abused the second verse entirely, and we have failed
to appreciate its true message to us.

I emphasise all this because knowing myself I think that such a
warning is very essential. We all of us, because of the effect that sin
has upon us, rather like reading verses like the second verse. People
always like a sermon or an address on a verse like that, and yet, if
we do not realise that John wrote the second verse in order to prepare the way for what he says in this third verse, then we have not
been using it aright. We have been using it for the time being to forget our trials and problems; we have been enjoying ourselves and
having a spiritual feast. Like Peter on the Mount of Transfiguration,
we have been rather tending to say, 'Let us make three tabernacles'
and spend the rest of our lives here in the wonder and enjoyment
of the feast of the glory. But we must not do that; we are not meant
to; we were taken up by John to the top of the mountain in order

that we might descend onto the plain and do this essential work that is waiting there for us—in exactly the same way as our Lord came down from the mountain to deal with the problem which had baffled and defeated his poor disciples. You and I, having had a vision of glory, have to come down and translate it into practise and put it into daily operation, and if it does not lead to that, then we are abusing the Scripture.

Now there is a logical connection between these two verses. John does not argue about it, he just states it—'every man that hath this hope in him purifieth himself, even as he is pure.' There is no need to discuss it; the one thing follows the other as the night follows the day. Therefore this third verse is one which comes to us as a very real and a very sure test; the extent to which I have really grasped the teaching of verse 2 is proved by the extent to which I implement verse 3. We can put it this way: it is what we are and what we do that really proclaims our belief and our profession.

That is the great theme in the epistle of James which has been so misunderstood—'faith without works is dead' (Jas 2:20)—and no one must dispute it. There is no disputation between James and John; both are saying the same thing—namely, that the profession of faith is of no avail unless it leads to this particular practise. Therefore we can put it the other way round with James and say that the real test of our profession is not so much what we are as what we do. Whatever I may have felt as I contemplated that second verse, if it does not lead me inevitably to the position which is described in the third verse, then it has been a false view because, according to John, this is pure logic. There is no discussion about it—'every man that hath . . .' He does not say, he *ought* to purify himself, he says that he *does*, and therefore it becomes a very thorough test of what we truly are.

In other words, is it not the case once more that our failure, most of us, is in the realm of belief, because this belief, says John, leads inevitably to that practise. Why do we therefore fail so much in practise? The answer, it seems to me, is that our belief is defective; if only we really did see ourselves as we are depicted in the New Testament, the problem of conduct would immediately be solved. So the real trouble with most Christian people is not so much in the realm of their conduct and practise as in the realm of their belief, and that is why the Church, whenever she puts too much emphasis upon conduct and behaviour and ethics, always leads eventually to a state and condition in which Christian people fail most of all in that respect.

This is a very subtle matter. Of course the tendency is for people to argue like this: 'Ah,' they say, 'there is not much point in talking to us about doctrine; you have to remind people of their practical duty.' So holiness teaching not infrequently becomes a constant repetition of certain duties which we are to carry out. I agree that we do have to do these things, but I say that the ultimate way of carrying out these duties, and really practising these things, is to have such a grasp and understanding of the doctrine that the practise becomes inevitable. And that is, of course, precisely what the New Testament always does. In other words, we cannot very well look at this verse without observing the way in which the New Testament always presents its teaching with regard to this whole question of holiness.

Here, I think, is a great corrective to what has so often taken place, and still does take place, in connection with this matter. Holiness, according to the New Testament, is an inevitable deduction from doctrine; it must never be regarded as something in and of itself. In other words, we must never approach the holy life simply in terms of living the holy life. And that, I think, is where the whole idea of monasticism and asceticism went astray. But the monastic conception of holiness is not, of course, confined to Roman Catholicism by any means. There are large numbers of evangelical people who clearly have a false idea of holiness; it is regarded as something in and of itself, something one has to go in for because of its nature, because it is a particular kind of life.

But that is never the teaching of the New Testament. Holiness is something that follows and is an inevitable deduction from doctrine, from an understanding of our position as Christian people. And especially, I think, we must admit that the New Testament presents its teaching and doctrine of holiness in terms of this great truth concerning the blessed hope. It is after it has told us what we are and who we are and of the hope that lies before us that the New

Testament brings in this doctrine of holiness and sanctification and Christian behaviour. I must therefore never talk about this idea of living the holy life because it is a good life in and of itself. Rather, my only reason for being holy is that I am a child of God and that I am destined for glory, and if I do not practise holiness in those terms I will sooner or later inevitably go astray.

That is, of course, what has happened with this other teaching of holiness. When you make holiness a thing of itself, you then produce your rules and regulations. You begin to pay too much attention to little details; you become legalistic without realising it; you become self-righteous because you have carried out your duties, and you forget the real objective for which you have originally set out.

Secondly, holiness is not something we are called upon to do in order that we may become something; it is something we are to do because of what we already are. Take this whole question of Lent.[1] There is a great deal of teaching on this subject which really amounts to this: that we are to be holy and live the holy life in order that we may become truly Christian. Every phase or aspect of the doctrine of justification by works really teaches that; so any suggestion we may have in ourselves that we are to deny ourselves certain things, that we are not to do certain things, and that we are to discipline ourselves in order that we may become Christian is a denial of the doctrine of justification by faith. But I am not to live a good and holy life in order that I may become a Christian; I am to live the holy life *because* I am a Christian. I am not to live this holy life in order that I may enter heaven; it is because I know I am going to enter heaven that I must live this holy life.

That is the emphasis here—'Every man that hath this hope in him purifieth himself, even as he is pure.' I am not to strive and sweat and pray in order that at the end I may enter into heaven. No; I start rather from the standpoint that I have been made a child of God by the grace of God in the Lord Jesus Christ. I am destined for heaven; I have an assurance that I have been called to go there and that God is going to take me there, and it is because I know this that I am preparing now. I must never regard that as contingent and uncertain in order that I may make it certain. It is exactly the other way round: it is because I know I am going to meet God that I must prepare to meet Him.

Thirdly, I must never conceive of holiness or sanctification as a kind of higher or happier or holier life which we are meant to enjoy as Christians and into which I ought to be entering. I must regard it rather as a life to which all Christians are inevitably called and which every Christian ought therefore automatically to be living. Now far too often the subject of holiness is handled like this: We are told that there is a wonderful life which you can live—a life with a capital L—a life of happiness and joy and peace. 'Why don't you enter into this life?' we are asked. Indeed, we are told that there are two types of Christians, the ordinary Christian and then the Christian who has had some kind of double blessing. You can be a Christian without that, but how foolish you are not to take this higher something which is there for you. I say there is no such definition in the New Testament at all. Holiness is something that is applicable to every Christian, not something which is some kind of extra. It is the norm of the Christian life, the life that everyone who has truly seen the doctrine is doing his or her utmost to live and to practise, with none of this division or dichotomy. All Christians, if they understand the doctrine truly, may be, and are, living this kind of life. It is not something in a separate category and department; it is something that flows out of the life that is in them; it is an inevitable expression of what they have received.

Or, lastly, let me put it like this: The holiness of which the New Testament speaks and the holy life, the life of sanctification which John talks of, is not so much something which we receive as a gift—it is rather something which we work out. Now here again I think this correction is needed. How often is the holiness doctrine presented in that form. We are told that as you have received your justification by faith as a gift, so you must now receive this gift of sanctification and holiness as a gift. So people get the idea that this life of holiness is something which comes to you perhaps in a meeting or a convention. You suddenly get it; you went to the meeting without it and then suddenly you got it.

But surely this is a denial of this very teaching which John is holding before us. No; the position is rather this—not that it suddenly comes to me and I receive some special or exceptional blessing; the position, rather, is that I am reminded of the doctrine, I am reminded that I am a child of God, I am told of the inheritance that awaits me. I have been given a glimpse of the vision of the glory that awaits me beyond death and the grave, and having seen it I am told, 'Now then, in the light of that, proceed to work this out, purify yourselves even as he is pure.' It is not a gift received but something which I must work out and put into practise. Consider how the Apostle Paul puts the same thing in Philippians 2:12-13: 'Work out your own salvation with fear and trembling: for it is God which worketh in you both to will and to do. . . .' And because of that you work it out. It is not some mystical experience that suddenly comes to us, but the outworking of the doctrine and the truth which we claim to believe.

Now all that is surely something of which we are reminded as we take a superficial glance at this third verse in its connection with the second verse, and we can put the teaching like this: If I really believe what that second verse has told me, if I really know that I am a child of God, with all that that means, if I believe and know that I am destined for eternal glory in the presence of God the Father, if I really believe that the Lord Jesus Christ is going to return again, to be 'manifested,' as John puts it, in this world as the King of kings and Lord of lords, if I believe He is coming to judge the world and to destroy everything that is evil and vile out of the universe as a whole, if I believe that I am going to be with Him in that glory, if furthermore I believe that I am going to see Him as he is, if I really believe that I am going to be like Him, that my very body shall be glorified, and that I shall be faultless and blameless and spend my eternity in His holy presence, if I really believe all that, says John, then of necessity this must follow.

What is it, then, that follows? The first thing that John tells us is that anyone who really believes that and has 'this hope in him *purifieth himself.*' Now it is very important that we should realise that 'him' does not refer to the man himself, but to Christ. John does not say, 'Every man that hath this hope within himself,' but 'Every man that hath this hope *in him*,' in the Christ of whom he has just been speaking in verse 2, in the Second Coming and in the power of our Lord to change our vile body so that it may be fashioned like unto His glorious body. It is the hope that is in Christ, in all that He is going to bring into the world and in all that He will do.

So, then, men and women who have this hope purify themselves, and this is a very interesting and a most important word. It is a very positive word; we must never think of it as negative. There is a difference between purifying and cleansing. We have considered 1 John 1:9,[2] 'If we confess our sins, he is faithful and just to forgive us our sins, and *to cleanse* us from all unrighteousness,' and the main difference between the two words is that between an external action and an internal action. To *cleanse* is to deliver, on the surface, from evil and pollution and all that is unworthy; *purification* is something that happens within, in the spirit and in the mind and in the essential nature. Therefore to purify means, in a sense, not only to get rid of the tarnishing effect of sin upon me, but also to avoid sin in my whole nature and in my whole being; so what I am told is that, as a Christian, I inevitably purify myself.

This means not only that I try to separate myself from the sins which I have committed in the past; it includes that, but it goes well beyond it. It means that with the whole of my being I shun sin, I avoid it. I have a desire within me to be like Christ; I am striving to be like the Lord Himself. It is not just that I do not sin, but that I am positively and actively pure even as He was pure. That is the whole idea of this word; it is a deeper and more profound word than just the idea of cleansing and of getting rid of the effects of sin upon the surface.

It is indeed perfectly expressed in just one phrase; people who are concerned about purifying themselves are those who want to be like the Lord Jesus Christ. They do not any longer merely think of just being a little bit better than obvious sinners in the world, nor a little bit better than they once were. Their whole idea is intensely positive and active. They say, 'I want my nature to be such that I shall love the light and hate the darkness instead of loving the darkness and hating the light. I want my whole being to be a positive desire to be like Christ and to be well-pleasing in His sight.' That, according to John, is the feeling of the men and women who truly understand this promise of the glory that yet awaits them.

Secondly, how do I do this? And here again we have to put it in the form perhaps of a criticism of a particular teaching. How am I to purify myself? Well, according to John, it is an active process, not a passive one; 'Every man that hath this hope in him *purifieth himself.*' He does not submit to purification; he purifies himself. The whole emphasis is upon the activity. In other words, the New Testament teaching about holiness is not one which tells me that all I have to do is to let myself go and to surrender myself, to give up effort and striving. It is not just telling me that all I have to do is to die and get rid of myself and forget myself and then life will come in. No! It is active, and I am told to purify myself 'even as he is pure.'

Now that is a doctrine which is not confined to John; you will find it everywhere in the New Testament. Take, for instance, the Apostle Paul in 2 Corinthians 7:1: 'Having these promises, let us cleanse ourselves from all filthiness of the flesh and spirit, perfecting holiness in the fear of God.' That is an identical statement with the verse that we are considering here. Let us *'cleanse ourselves,'* not submit passively to some process which will cleanse us. Take also Hebrews 6:11-12 where we are exhorted to show some diligence in this matter of 'the full assurance of hope unto the end'; we are not to be slothful, but, like those who have gone before us, we must be diligent and press on and strive to perfect ourselves because of the hope that is set before us.

There are many other terms in the New Testament which suggest the same thing. Take those words which are used by the Apostle Paul in various places: 'Mortify therefore your members which are upon the earth' (Col 3:5). I have to do that; these members will not agree to be mortified; *I* have to take them, and I have to punish my body. I am enabled to do that by the Holy Spirit who has been given to me; yes, and that is included in the fact that I am a child of God. I have been born again, I have received a new nature, and the Holy Spirit is in me. Therefore, because of that, I must do this, I must purify myself even as He is pure.

But, still more in detail, how am I to do this? Well, this is the way in which the New Testament indicates that the process must be followed up: I purify myself by considering Him, by looking at Him and His perfect life; that is the pattern I am to follow. We are

reminded of that by the Apostle Paul. God has called us that we
may be 'conformed to the image of his Son' (Rom 8:29). So if that
is God's plan and purpose for me, then the first thing I must do is
to look at the Lord Jesus Christ, to look at the way He conducted
Himself in this life and world. I am to be like Him, so I consider
Him. I realise that is what I am destined for, so I begin to put it into
practise.

The other way in which it is put is this: we are told to 'set your
affection on things above, not on things on the earth' (Col 3:2).
Again observe the activity—*set* your affections on things above.
Read your Bible every day; meditate upon eternity and the glory
that awaits you; think about these things; reflect upon the glory. Do
not let your mind be set upon things that are on the earth; deliberately refuse to do so.

Or consider again: 'for our light affliction, which is but for a
moment, worketh for us a far more exceeding and eternal weight
of glory; while we look not at the things which are seen, but at the
things which are not seen: for the things which are seen are temporal; but the things which are not seen are eternal' (2 Cor 4:17-18).
We must look at the things that are not seen, so we meditate upon
them; and having looked at Him and having followed Him, and
while we are looking and setting our affection on the things which
are above, we must do our utmost to see that vision of glory more
and more clearly. We must not love the world. We must mortify our
members that are upon the earth. We must crucify the flesh. And
as we do all these things we shall be purifying ourselves even as He
is pure. That is how it is to be done.

Then, lastly, what are the encouragements and the motives for
Christians to purify themselves in this way? I think they are quite
self-evident. Is it not a matter of what we might call Christian common sense? If I believe that I am a child of God and that I am really
going to heaven and to glory, if I believe that this uncertain life of
mine may suddenly come to an end at any moment and then I shall
be with the Lord in all the glory and perfection, is it surely not common sense that I ought to be preparing myself for that? Is it not
hopelessly illogical and unreasonable to go on living in antithesis
to that to which I am called? It is not a matter to be argued; there

is a sense in which we should never have to appeal to Christian people to live a holy life. What John does is what we all ought to do.
If we believe this, if we claim this, then it is consistent, it is a matter
of common sense, it is a matter of logic, it is a matter of being rea-
sonable that we should do so.

But there are further inducements given us in the Bible.
Because of our frailty, another great reason for purifying ourselves
is that we may not find ourselves feeling ashamed when we arrive
in glory. John has told us that in the previous chapter and the
twenty-eighth verse: 'And now, little children, abide in him; that
when he shall appear, we may have confidence, and not be ashamed
before him at his coming.' This means that if you are a child of God,
you are going to see Him when he comes; you will see Him as He
is, for the first time. You will really understand what your salvation
meant to Him and what it cost Him when you look into His face
and into His blessed eyes. 'And if you do not want to feel ashamed,'
says John, 'if you do not want to feel you are a cad and that you
have been a fool because you have kept your gaze fixed upon the
little things of earth with their foulness and their unworthiness, then
prepare for the vision now; be ready for its coming, and avoid that
sense of shame.'

But that is negative. An even stronger reason for purifying ourselves is that we all ought to have a positive desire to be like Him.
We ought to be filled with a yearning and a longing to live this glorious, wondrous life that Christ has made possible for us by His
death and resurrection. Should not we all be animated by a desire
to please Him if we really believe He came from heaven to earth?
If we really believe that He suffered the agony of the cross and shed
His holy blood that we might be redeemed and rescued, if we really
believe that and love Him, should not our greatest desire be to
please Him?

That is the reason for holy living, that is the New Testament
appeal for holiness; it is an appeal to our sense of honour, to our
sense of love and gratitude. But if you want a final appeal, let me
appeal to you in terms of the time element. 'He that hath this hope
in him,' those who believe they are going to see Him and be like
Him and be with Him, purify themselves even as He is pure, and

they feel there is not a moment to be lost. Oh, the unworthiness that is in me! Not only the sins I have committed and still commit, but the evil nature, the unworthiness in me, all these things which I have to mortify. There is so much to be done, and time is uncertain. We do not have a moment to spare or to waste. We may find ourselves with Him, facing Him, at any moment.

That is the spirit of the New Testament—people pressing on towards the mark, straining at the leash, looking forward, going forward with all their might. And because they are looking at the vision of glory for which they are destined, they are pressing on towards it and towards Him, forgetting the things that are behind, redeeming the time, buying up the opportunity, using every second because of the certainty that they will see Him as He is and that they will be like Him. God grant that this inevitable logic may be plain and clear to each and every one.

4

The Sinless Saviour

And ye know that he was manifested to take away our sins;
and in him is no sin.

1 JOHN 3:5

W e should read verses 4 to 10 to get this verse in context, because it is essential that we should bear all this in mind as we come to look together at the message and at the statement of this particular fifth verse. We see that here in this verse, and in this entire section, the Apostle is continuing the discussion of what he had begun to deal with in the third verse. In the first two chapters he has written about our fulness of joy as Christians, about our fellowship with God and how that fellowship is to be maintained. That is his first great theme. Then, you remember, here in this chapter he is dealing with the whole position of the Christian as a child of God, and this is his second great appeal. He has shown us that another great secret of living this Christian life thoroughly in this world is to realise this whole standing and position of ours.

But here he goes on to his other theme, and the first thing he wants to emphasise again is that this whole question of righteousness and of holy living is an essential and vital part of this whole position and of our understanding of the position, and he feels that he must make this so abundantly plain and clear that we can never go astray about it. He again warns them: 'Little children, let no man deceive you' (v 7). As there are heresies that would lead us astray

49

about the person of our Lord and His work, so there are heresies with regard to sin, and that is the subject with which he deals in this great and familiar passage.

Now it is again interesting to observe in passing that his method of handling this whole question of holiness and righteousness is so typical, not only of him, but also of all the New Testament writers. The appeal for holiness, as we have seen, is always made in terms of doctrine. Holiness must never be isolated; it is always deduced from something that has gone before. It is an inevitable consequence of a true understanding of our position in Christ Jesus. And John goes on to show us once more that that is his method. Holiness is a matter of working out what we claim to believe; therefore failure in practise does suggest a failure truly to understand the doctrine, and is an indication that there is something essentially and fundamentally wrong with one's view of the Christian life.

Now the particular failure with which he is concerned here is the failure really to understand the nature of sin. There are many tendencies with regard to this; John has already dealt with one of them in chapter 1,[1] where he showed us the danger of the false perfectionist ideas. People have such an inadequate view of sin that they think they are already perfect; they regard sin in terms of particular actions and so fail to realise its pollution as well as its power within them.

Now here he seems to be pointing out quite a different danger and heresy with regard to sin—that of regarding it lightly, dismissing it in some inadequate way as if it were something that really does not matter very much so long as one is a Christian. But John is careful to guard very strongly against that. He says, 'Whosoever committeth sin transgresseth also the law: for sin is the transgression of the law' (v 4). 'You must be right, therefore,' says the Apostle, 'about this whole question of the real nature of sin, because if you are wrong there, you must be wrong on your doctrine of salvation, and then you are wrong everywhere.' And so his great emphasis at this point is that sin is lawlessness, the breaking of God's law, rebellion against God, disobedience, a failure to live our lives as God would have us live them.

That is the very essence of sin. It must not be thought of as just a sort of weakness or failure on our part; it must not be regarded as some sort of bestial past which we have not yet sloughed off. No, John says, sin is not negative, it is positive. It is the transgression of the law; it is disobedience to God and His holy will with respect to us. 'So if you fail to realise this,' says the Apostle in effect, 'then it does just show that you are muddled and confused in your thinking about the whole principle of the coming of the Lord Jesus Christ into this world. And it seems clear that your whole conception of salvation must be entirely false and erroneous'—and then he proceeds to deal with that.

'Man's essential trouble,' says the Apostle, 'is that he is guilty and condemned by the law of God. Sin was introduced into this world by the devil; the devil came at the very beginning and tempted man to disobey God. That is *lawlessness*: he tempted him to break God's holy law, and man in his folly listened to him and did so. That is a part of the work of the devil, and its effect has been to make us break the law of God and to render us guilty in the sight of God and His holy law. There we are, under the wrath of God, meriting and awaiting punishment. That is the position,' says John, 'so that if you do not view your sin in that way, then it is quite obvious that you cannot understand anything else because the Lord Jesus Christ was manifested, or appeared, in this world because of that.'

John, you notice, makes two separate statements with regard to the object of the coming of our Lord Jesus Christ: 'Ye know that he was manifested to take away our sins' (v 5), and 'For this purpose the Son of God was manifested, that he might destroy the works of the devil' (v 8). That is the whole purpose, and we must view His coming in the light of those two great statements.

So let us consider now this first statement in verse 5. Let us pause and ask this most vital question: why did the Son of God ever come into this world? We know that He was 'manifested,' and we have reminded ourselves how John likes to put it in this way. He says, 'That which was from the beginning, which we have heard, which we have seen with our eyes, which we have looked upon, and our hands have handled, of the Word of life; (for the life was *manifested*, and we have seen it . . .)' (1:1-2), and here he says it again. So why was this?

When we think about the Lord Jesus Christ and especially about His death on that cross on Calvary's hill, what is its purpose?[2] Is it just something about which we sentimentalise? What does it represent to us? We have to ask, Why was the Son of God born into this world as a baby in Bethlehem? What is the meaning of the Incarnation? Why did He ever leave the courts of heaven and come in that way into this world? Then, why did He spend His life as He did those first thirty years? What is the meaning of His preaching and His teaching and His miracles? What is the purpose of His life here on earth, and above all, why that cross? Why this manifestation and demonstration; why the burial and the rising again and the appearance and the Ascension? What is the explanation of it all?

That is the question that John answers here, and let me first put the answer in its negative form. Our Lord did not only come to give us a revelation of God, though that is a part of the purpose. He said, 'He that hath seen me hath seen the Father' (John 14:9), and we also read, 'No man hath seen God at any time; the only begotten Son, which is in the bosom of the Father, he hath declared him' (John 1:18). But that is not all, though He has indeed revealed the Father and has come to do that. In the same way, He has not only come to teach us about God. There *is* incomparable teaching there, such as the world has never known before and has not known since, but He did not come only to do that. There is also, of course, the example of His life, a matchless one, but He has not come only to give us an example of how we should live in this world. He is not just a teacher or a moral exemplar; he has not come to give us some kind of picture as to the nature and being of God. All that is there, but that is not the real reason, says John.

He has really come, he says, because of our sins, because of the predicament and the position of men and women, because of this whole question of law. He has not come only to instruct us and to give us encouragement in our endeavour and a great example. No, there is a fundamental problem at the back of it all, and that is our relationship to God in the light of God's holy law. We are under the law, and He has really come because of that. 'Ye know that he was manifested to take away our sins; and in him is no sin.' So it is only as we understand this whole question of sin in terms of law that we can possibly understand why He came and especially why He ever went to that cruel death upon the cross. He came, as the New Testament tells us everywhere, because in a sense He had to come if we were to be delivered. He came because there was no other way whereby we could be redeemed and rescued. He came 'to seek and to save that which was lost' (Luke 19:10). He came because of this whole question of what sin has done to us and the position in which it has landed us with respect to God and His holy law. And here John puts all that to us in this particularly striking manner.

So let us see what God has done with regard to this predicament in which we find ourselves. The first thing John tells us is that we do not understand the Lord Jesus Christ properly apart from ourselves and our sinful condition, apart from this whole question of the law. So the first statement that John makes is that He Himself is without sin. There was no sin in the Lord Jesus Christ; He was perfect, spotless, blameless; He was born without sin. So, you see, it is looking at Him in terms of law that really shows us that we must not only accept the biblical statement with regard to the virgin birth of our Lord, but also why this is essential. The Holy Ghost came upon Mary, and He was born. He became man; He took unto Himself this human nature, yes, but He was without sin. In the miracle that took place there He received the perfect human nature.

'In him is no sin.' We have to start with that for the reasons which will emerge as we continue, but that is always the starting point. There can be no true view of salvation and of the redemption that is possible for us in the Lord Jesus Christ unless we are right about the person. That is why John, you remember, used such strong and striking language in chapter 2[3] when he talked about those people who were leading them astray by denying the person of our Lord. 'Those antichrists,' he said, 'are liars, and they must be called such because they are robbing us of the whole of our salvation.' If we are wrong about the person, we shall be wrong everywhere. So as we look at this person we are reminded again in this verse that here is one who has been in this world of ours with all its sin and its shame, but who was without sin. He 'was in all points tempted like as we are, yet without sin' (Heb 4:15). He remains there unique and separate. He is the Son of God, and none other. He is not just a great moral teacher, nor just a great religious genius. He is not one who has gone a little bit further than all others in this quest for God and for truth. No, He is the Son of God incarnate– 'in him is no sin.' – ultimately what sets him apart

But not only was there no sin in Him and in His birth–He committed no act of sin. He always honoured God's holy law; He obeyed it fully and carried it out perfectly. God gave His law to man. He intended that that law should be carried out, that it should be honoured and obeyed. Let me go further and say this: no one can ever be with God and spend eternity with Him unless they have honoured the law. God's law must be kept, and without fulfilling it there is no fellowship with Him and no hope of spending eternity with Him. And here is One who has kept the law, who lived in this world exactly as you and I have to live in it. He worked as a carpenter. He had been a child, yet no one was ever able to convict Him of sin. He defied them to do so; He rendered a perfect obedience to God and to His holy law. What God has demanded from man and man has failed to do, here is One who does it. He fulfils it. 'In him is no sin'; He has satisfied the law of God. He has actively and positively obeyed it and rendered it fully.

This, I say again, is something which is absolutely essential to our salvation, for the problem of man with respect to God is not only the problem of the guilt of sin. Merely to be forgiven is not enough; we have to keep the law of God. Notice how Paul puts that in Romans 8, where he says that in Christ Jesus God has 'condemned sin in the flesh: that the righteousness of the law might be fulfilled in us' (vv 3-4). We have to keep that law, but we have not kept it; we cannot do so, and we can only keep it in Him. He has kept the law for us; He has rendered this obedience and satisfied this demand of the law of God.

But let us go on another step. In addition to that He has dealt with the problem of the guilt of our sin, because He has provided a perfect sacrifice and offering for our sin. In the Old Testament we read of all the burnt offerings and sacrifices, those types and shadows which God gave the ancient people of Israel in order to show them how sacrifice must be made for sin. 'Without shedding of blood is no remission' of sin (Heb 9:22), and the sacrifice and offering had to be perfect. It had to be 'without blemish'—that was all a type and a shadow of the perfect offering. It must be human, it must be a man, and here is the perfect sacrifice for sin, for 'in him is no sin.'

You see, it is all in terms of the law. While the law demands perfection, it cannot admit any blemish; you cannot offer a perfect sacrifice for sin if there is any defect. If the Lord Jesus Christ had sinned once, He could no longer have been that perfect offering for our sins; but 'in him is no sin,' and therefore He is the sacrifice. 'There was no other good enough to pay the price of sin.'⁴ He has come in the flesh, He has been born as a man, and yet He is without sin; therefore He can offer Himself, and it is a perfect offering.

And that leads us to the next step. By doing that, says John, He has taken away our sins—'Ye know he was manifested to take away our sins.' We are reminded of the words of John the Baptist when he looked at Jesus at the beginning and said, 'Behold the Lamb of God, which taketh away the sin of the world' (John 1:29). That is the meaning of Good Friday, that is the explanation of the Cross—our sins have been laid upon Him, and they have been dealt with there in Him; He has taken them away. Your sins and mine do not any longer belong to us; they have been taken from us; He has made Himself responsible for them. The ideas here are those of the lamb that was slain, and also of the scapegoat, on whom was placed the sin of the people and then he was sent away into the wilderness (Lev 16). That is what the Lord Jesus Christ has done for us. That is why He came, that is the whole purpose of His Incarnation, that is why He staggered up Golgotha, that is why He was nailed to the tree. He is bearing away my sins and yours.

But it was the law that demanded that; it would never have happened were it not for the law, and that is why we must never regard sin as something light and trivial. That is why we must never refer to it as some sort of weakness and say, 'It does not matter very much now that I am a Christian.' Sin is a transgression of the law. It is such a terrible thing that it led to the death of Christ, and one sin is enough to demand that. 'Let no man deceive you,' says John.

Do you not see that if you are wrong in your outlook upon sin, then it just means that you have never seen its enormity, you have never seen the problem it has created for man and, in a sense, I say it with reverence, for God Himself. This holy law, this expression of God's being and character, condemns sin utterly. The condemnation is death, and without the sacrificial atonement there is no forgiveness. But, wonder of wonders, God has provided and found the way there on the cross. My sins are no longer imputed to me, they are no longer on record against me, and as my sinful story is there revealed in the Book of Life, it is all cancelled by Christ.

So those who believe that cannot regard sin lightly. They cannot say that a righteous life is a matter of indifference. Those who really believe this and are governed by it and who are truly holy in the New Testament sense are not holy just because they believe it is a 'good life.' They see it all in the light of the law of God and of the cross and of the Christ who came as the Lamb of God; the argument and the logic are inescapable. So the New Testament does not just appeal to us to be holy for the sake of being holy—it puts it into this context.

But lastly, there is one further step. It is obvious that in this context and setting, when John says that 'he was manifested to take away our sins,' he is not stopping at the guilt of our sins, for salvation goes beyond that. We are delivered from the guilt—it is the first thing that is essential—but, thank God, the process does not stop there. He delivers us also from the power and from the pollution of sin. His work is such that he takes away our sin in a more vital sense. We are growing in grace and in the knowledge of the Lord; we are increasingly being made to conform to the image of His Son. We are being delivered—we have been, we are, and we shall be ultimately. The glorification is coming when He will take away our sin altogether, so that we shall be blameless and faultless and spotless and perfect in His holy presence.

That hymn which tells us, 'There was no other good enough to pay the price of sin' also tells us this: 'He died that we might be forgiven'; yes, but 'He died to make us good' is equally true. The Apostle Paul, writing to Titus, says: '[He] gave himself for us, that he might redeem us from all iniquity, and purify unto himself a peculiar [separate] people, zealous of good works' (Titus 2:14).

So we must never separate sanctification from justification; we must never separate holiness and forgiveness; we must never talk about a kind of series of separate blessings; all is one—it all belongs together. And it is all a matter of this law that condemns us and from which he delivers us through the cross and by the gift of new life. He went to that cruel death on the cross not only that you and I might have pardon. Thank God, that does come out of it, that is the first thing. But He did it really to separate, to put aside, a people for Himself as an especial treasure and possession, who, as Paul puts it, should be 'zealous of good works,' who would live a righteous, holy life, a people who would be a demonstration and manifestation to the whole world, and, yes, to the principalities and powers in heavenly places, of this wondrous Christ of God who has been able to do so much and to make so much of sinful, fallen men and women.

That, then, is what we know. 'Ye know that he was manifested to take away our sins; and in him is no sin.' I do hope that you know that you are forgiven, that the guilt of your sin has been taken away. I trust you know also that He is delivering you increasingly from the power of sin and from its pollution and that you look forward to 'that blessed hope, and the glorious appearing of the great God and our Saviour Jesus Christ' (Titus 2:13), when He shall finally come back and wind up the affairs of earth and of time and destroy evil in its every manifestation and usher in that eternal glory in which we, as the children of God, shall share.

God grant that that may be our position and our experience.

5

Victory over the Devil

For this purpose the Son of God was manifested, that he might destroy the works of the devil.

1 JOHN 3:8

This is the second of the two great statements which John makes in this first section of chapter 3 with regard to the whole object and purpose of the coming of the Son of God into this world of time. We have been considering the first statement in verse 5: 'And ye know that he was manifested to take away our sins; and in him is no sin.'

These two statements together remind us of what the Fathers were very fond of describing as the 'Drama of Redemption.' This is a very good phrase, a phrase which helps us to look at the gospel in the right way and manner and which reminds us immediately of the very essence of the gospel message. It is astounding that in spite of the records which we have in the New Testament, our tendency always is to turn the gospel into a point of view, into an idea and a teaching, and to forget that it was first and foremost a series of events and of facts which actually took place.

That, it seems to me, is the inevitable result of sin. The Apostle Paul tells us in his letters to the Corinthians and to the Colossians that he was aware of that very subtle danger. He was always afraid of somehow or another nullifying the whole message of the Cross by turning it into a philosophy. For the very essence of the gospel message is that it is not first and foremost a teaching, but a proclamation, an announcement of certain things that have happened. When you read the book of Acts you will find that the first preachers travelled around and were heralds of the message. They told that ancient world of certain things which had happened; they talked about a person, and they reported what had happened to Him. And with a very special emphasis, they told people of the amazing fact of the Resurrection; how this person, Jesus of Nazareth—who had been completely misunderstood, not only by the common people, but by the rulers and elders of the people—how He had been put to death. But, they said, God had raised Him from the dead, and He had manifested Himself to them, His chosen witnesses, and to certain other people. And they told how, after He had spent forty days on the earth, they had seen Him rising into the heavens; and now they were preaching in the power of the amazing gift He had sent to them, a person they called the Holy Spirit.

And we are reminded of all that by these words that we are now considering. We see that our Lord did not come into the world only to teach. He did do that, and He gave incomparable teaching, but before we ever come to consider His teaching—at any rate before it can be of any value to us at all in any practical sense—we must first realise what He came primarily to do. 'For this purpose the Son of God was manifested,' not that He might teach us, not that He might give us a glorious example to follow, not that He might give us some transcendent idea which would illumine our minds and thrill us—not at all!

He came, He was manifested, He appeared that He might 'destroy the works of the devil.' He came to do something, and our salvation is dependent upon what He Himself has done. He does not just come and call upon us to do something. The first and the most essential message of the gospel is to ask us to recognise and then to receive what He has done. That is why salvation is a gift, and that is why the business of preaching is to offer men and women this gift of salvation and to hold it before them.

And that is what John here emphasises in these two striking

statements. Now you observe that in both instances he puts it in terms of sin. Whether we like it or not, that is always the context and the background to this presentation of the truth. Our Lord really came, says John, and had to come, because of sin, and that is what he is outlining in this whole section.

First of all he looks at sin as it brings us under the condemnation of God's holy law, and secondly he looks at sin as it puts us under the dominion and under the government of Satan and makes us become a part of Satan's work. 'He that committeth sin is of the devil; for the devil sinneth from the beginning . . .,' but 'Whosoever is born of God doth not commit sin. . . . In this the children of God are manifest, and the children of the devil' (vv 8–10). So there are two ways of looking at sin and at the effects of sin on us.

The first way is to see that sin is unrighteous, that it is a transgression of the law, and that *sin* means we are violating God's holy will for us and God's holy purpose with respect to us. But this is the other way: 'To continue in a life of sin and evil,' says John, 'is just to identify yourself at once with the devil and his ways and with everything that belongs to him,' and it is that which is emphasised in this eighth verse.

Now two things stand out very clearly in the particular way in which John puts it. The first is that our Lord came into this world to wage a great fight; He entered into a mighty battle. The second is the way in which he was victorious in the fight, the way in which He overcame for us the adversary and his approaches. That is the thing that is celebrated especially on Easter Day;[1] this is the day that reminds us of Christ's victory, of a fact. It is not a day that reminds us of certain principles in life. You often hear people thank God for this whole 'principle of resurrection,' how the flowers begin to appear, and how the trees and life come into being in the Spring. Now, that has nothing to do with this blessed message of the Resurrection. We are concerned about a fact, not a principle of nature, and the fact is that there, in the Resurrection, our Lord ultimately established His conquest over the devil.

So realising this, realising, as John says, that Christ came that He might destroy the works of the devil, let us begin by considering this 'adversary,' as he is described, the devil. The Son of God

came because there was a certain state and condition in this world
that had been produced by the devil. Now whether we like it or not,
the fact is that the whole drama of redemption, as it is outlined in
the Bible, simply cannot be understood at all unless you accept the
Biblical doctrine with regard to the devil. It is an essential part of
this message; it is here from the very beginning and right through
to the end.

And this is the Biblical teaching. The explanation of the problem of mankind and the whole state of our world is to be traced
back to this fact about the devil. According to the Bible, God made
the world perfect; so what has gone wrong with it? And here is the
answer. Someone, who is described in various terms and to whom
various names are given in the Bible, came and spoke to the man
and the woman whom God had placed in that perfect world. He is
called 'Lucifer,' 'the son of the morning' and 'the god of this world.'
He is called 'the serpent,' 'the prince of the power of the air,' and
'the strong man armed.' There are various names given in the
Scriptures, but they all describe the same person. And according to
this teaching, this is the explanation of evil and of sin and of all our
miseries in this world. The devil came and spoke to man, and he
enticed him to sin; so man went against God; and the result of all
that is the state of the world as it has been from the moment that
man fell.

Summing it up we can put it like this: This world has become
the kingdom of Satan; Satan has produced certain results which we
shall consider together—these 'works of the devil' about which our
text speaks. And our Lord and Saviour Jesus Christ came into this
world because of that fact. Men and women need to be delivered
from the law of God that condemns them; and thereby they need
to be delivered from the punishment of their sin. But they also need
to be delivered out of this kingdom of the devil, out of the kingdom
of Satan; and they need to be translated into the kingdom of God.
And the Son of God came, according to this whole biblical teaching, because of that kingdom which Satan had established. Christ
came into this world in order to conquer Satan and his kingdom
and in order to introduce His own kingdom. So what you have in
the Bible, in a sense, is the story of the conflict of the two king-

doms—the kingdom of God and the kingdom of the devil, the kingdom of Christ and the kingdom of Satan, the kingdom of light and the kingdom of darkness, the kingdom of the Son of God and the kingdom of this world. It is the conflict between heaven and hell and between light and darkness—that is the Biblical terminology.

Now that being the statement in general, let us look at it a little more in particular. Evil has come in through the devil, this great adversary of God and of man. So what are the works of the devil; what has he been trying to do? Well, his great endeavour is to separate men and women from God; that is what he is really concerned to bring about. He was jealous of man's obedience and allegiance to God, and in his very hatred of God his one desire is to ruin, to mar and to destroy the glorious works of God in this world.

Now he has proceeded to do that work, according to the Scriptures, in a very deceptive manner. He is often described as 'subtle,' and he is also described as a 'liar.' You will find that our Lord Himself in speaking of him says of him that he is 'a liar, and the father of it' (John 8:44), and all his works have just been, in some shape or form, the repetition of some kind of a lie. He has persuaded men and women to believe and to accept these various lies, and all our unhappiness in this world is the result of our folly in believing the subtlety and the lies of Satan. That is the essence of the biblical explanation of our predicament. There would be no unhappiness in the world but for this. Evil and sin, according to the Bible, would not be here. There would be no drunkenness, no quarrelling; there would be no infidelity and divorce, there would be no threats of war, and no confusion and disturbances, were it not that people in their folly have believed the lie of Satan.

There are various forms which that lie has taken. The essence of the lie which Satan has persuaded man to believe is the lie about God Himself; it is the old lie about God's attitude towards man. God made man and woman perfect and gave them a perfect world to live in; and God gave them the supreme privilege of holding communion with Him. He gave them everything that they needed. They did not have to work to make a living at the beginning; there was the fruit, and they had but to take it and enjoy it. God showered His blessings upon them, but the devil came and said, 'Are you foolish enough to believe that God really loves you? Can't you see He is making slaves of you? This one thing He is prohibiting you is just a mark of His hostility with respect to you.' So the lie of Satan is the lie against God at the beginning. And is that not true of all of us? Have we not known in our hearts that when things go wrong, our first hatred is a feeling of hatred against God? This enmity against God is the work of Satan, who lies to us about God, about His attitude towards us, about His love to us, and about His concern for our happiness and well-being.

And that in turn leads to the second lie which is, as we have just seen, the lie about God's holy will. God gives laws to man, and He gives us these laws for our good and for our benefit. It is because God made men and women that He knows what is good for them, and when He gave them conditions at the beginning it was for their good. But they did not see it, and they believed the lie of Satan that the laws of God were against them. How fond people are of saying that the gospel is narrow, and how many reject it for that reason— as if to live a life like the Lord Jesus Christ is to be so small and petty and narrow! No, that is the lie about God's law, God's way of life, God's holiness. By nature we all instinctively dislike the holy life because we believe the lie of sin.

Then, of course, the next lie was the lie about the consequences of sin and of disobedience. 'God has told you,' said Satan to the first man and woman, 'that if you disobey and break His law, then certain consequences will come upon you and you will die. Don't believe Him,' said Satan. 'If you do this which is prohibited, your eyes will be opened and you will become like gods. God doesn't want you to be like Him, so He is holding you down and repressing you. But do this thing and I tell you, you will be greater than you are now.' So he lied to them about the consequences of sin and disobedience, and that produced all the terrible consequences of the Fall.

And Satan still does this self-same thing. He whispers to us all and tells us to disobey God and to break His holy law; and he assures us that we can do that with impunity and nothing will go wrong. And in our folly we all tend to believe him. But later we come to understand that the way of the transgressor is hard and that though for a moment we may go against God and imagine we have wonderful freedom, sooner or later we begin to discover that 'whatsoever a man soweth, that shall he also reap' and 'he that soweth to his flesh shall of the flesh reap corruption' (Gal 6:7-8). The devil lies about the consequences, and men and women in their folly believe the lie.

So the question arises, Why does Satan do all this? Why did he do it at the beginning, and why has he continued to do so? The answer is that he was anxious to get the man and woman under his own power and dominion. His motive and desire was to make them sin and to live a sinful life, and he succeeded. They did sin, and they began to live that sinful life. Not only that, Satan is also anxious to prevent us from living the godly and good life. He is anxious to rob us of all the benefits that God has for us, and the result of all this is that, having listened to the lie of Satan, we have put ourselves under his domination.

Our Lord put that in a very memorable picture when he said, 'When a strong man armed keepeth his palace, his goods are in peace' (Luke 11:21). 'That is the result of sin,' says our Lord. 'You have made yourselves the slaves and the serfs of Satan. You are in the stronghold, the castle, of Satan, and he won't let you get out; nor will he let you live the godly, holy life. If you try, he will strike you down; you are under his power and dominion.' And that, according to the Bible, is the whole state of the world today. The results of the activity and the works of Satan are that men and women are under the rule of Satan. They have disobeyed God and offended Him. They have broken God's holy law and have been condemned. They had been told what not to do, but they deliberately did it; so they are left with no excuse and are under the wrath of God.

Not only that, their very nature is sinful—they prefer evil to good. There is an instinct in them that takes them astray; there is that within them which lusts and gives way to passion. Their very nature has become twisted and perverted, and as a result of this, they experience misery and unhappiness. Indeed their world has become a place of woe and trouble. It is no use pretending otherwise; it is a fact, and we in this century have experienced it in an exceptional manner—wars and confusion and despair and unhappiness. All this is the result of the work of Satan.

And standing at the end of it all is the fact of death itself. By listening to the lie of Satan, men and women have put themselves under the power of death. As the Scripture is so fond of teaching us, whether we explain it away to our own satisfaction or not, we all in this world by nature live under the tyranny and the fear of death. It is ever present, always advancing towards us, spoiling our greatest and best pleasures. It is the last enemy, it is inevitable, and it is tyrannising the whole of life.

Finally, and perhaps the greatest of all the results of the works of the devil, is the state of the world apart from Christ. That is the sort of world into which Christ came, in which the Son of God was manifested. He appeared in a world that was under the dominion of Satan, a world miserable, unhappy, sinful, perverted, alienated from God, under the wrath of God and with death ever facing it. So why did He ever leave the courts of heaven and the glory which He shared with his Father from the beginning; why did He come?

Here is the answer: 'For this purpose the Son of God was manifested, that he might destroy the works of the devil.' Thank God for this message! By doing all that He has come to do, the Son of God has fulfilled the ancient promise which was given to man and woman immediately after the Fall. Into the chaos that resulted from evil and sin the promise came: The seed of the woman shall bruise the serpent's head. 'Satan has got you down, the serpent has misled you in his subtlety,' said God to Adam and Eve, 'but it is all right—I will send someone who will bruise his head, the seed of the woman' (Gen 3:15)—and that is the Lord Jesus Christ. So we must view His coming into this world in terms of all that Satan had done and had produced. Christ has come to fight it; He has come with a mighty sword. 'Think not,' he said, 'that I am come to send peace on earth: I came not to send peace, but a sword' (Matt 10:34). He has come to destroy and to undo the works of the devil.

And He has done it like this: His very incarnation undoes the lie of Satan, for if the Incarnation tells us one thing more than anything else, it is that God is love and that God has loved us with an everlasting love. 'God is against you,' says the devil. 'God hates you, and He delights to keep you down. He wants to rob you of everything that is yours by right.' 'No,' says the Incarnation, 'God is love.' Here is a world that has rebelled against God. It spat into His holy face; in arrogance it lifted itself up against Him; it said, 'I have a right to be equal with God.' Now, a world like that deserves nothing but punishment; it deserves perdition. Yet into that very world that I have been describing God sent His Son–'God so loved the world, that he gave his only begotten Son' (John 3:16). The babe in Bethlehem is a denial of the lie of Satan. He says, 'I am here because God loves you.' He has come to undo the works of the devil; He has come to contradict the lies of Satan, and His very appearing and coming, let me emphasise it again, is in itself an undoing of the original lie–it is proof that God loves us.

But look at His life, look at His way of living. Think of Him as He stands before us in the Gospels; look at that perfect, spotless life. Can you still say the holy life is a small, narrow one? Do you believe He was just an apology of a man because He did not drink and curse and swear and gamble and do the various things that men claim are 'life' in a real sense today? Look at Him; look at Him in all His virtue and all His utter sinlessness. He has established there, once and for ever, that the only life worthy to be called life is one which is lived in utter, absolute conformity to the commands of the holy God; in His life He denies the lie of the devil.

Listen, then, to His teaching as He exposes in its utter depths the evil nature of sin and of wrongdoing. Listen to His interpretation and exposition of the law of Moses. In the Sermon on the Mount, for instance, He says, 'You do not have to *commit* sin; just to look with lust in your eyes is sufficient' (Matt 5:28); that is the exposure of sin. He gets down to the depth and says that 'out of the heart proceed evil thoughts, murders, adulteries' and other evils (Matt 15:19). He exposes the perversion and the twistedness of evil–the foulness and ugliness of sin. In His teaching He is undoing the lie, the works of Satan.

But watch Him as He works His miracles and His mighty deeds; what is He doing there? Well, He is just doing this great work of destroying or undoing the works of Satan. Take the occasion when He healed a poor woman who was not only a cripple but was utterly doubled up and indeed had been like that for eighteen years. He spoke to her, and immediately she stood erect. What has He done here? This in effect is what He says: 'Satan has bound this woman for eighteen years, and I am undoing the chains which Satan has forged around her; I am setting her free.' (Luke 13:10-13). 'When a strong man armed keepeth his palace, his goods are in peace: But when a stronger than he shall come upon him, and overcome him, he taketh from him all his armor wherein he trusted, and divideth his spoils' (Luke 11:21-22). He sets the captive free. That is what He is doing in His miracles; He is undoing the works of Satan. He is breaking the chains that had been forged in various ways; He is setting the captive at liberty.

Look thus right through His life and then come to His death. What is He doing on that cross on Calvary's hill? He is dealing there with the guilt; He is undoing there the condemnation of the lie. He is wiping away the guilt; He is setting us right with God; He is reconciling us to God. He has undone the condemnation of sin that results from listening to the lie of Satan.

Let us come to the Resurrection. There He is giving us the final proof that God is pleased with His work; He is proclaiming to us that we can be sure of our salvation. There He says, 'Now is the judgment of this world: now shall the prince of this world be cast out' (John 12:31). He is showing there that He has conquered even death itself, the very 'last enemy' as Paul described it (1 Cor 15:26). There, by rising from the dead, He has established that He has conquered every single enemy. On His cross He has exposed Satan himself and all the principalities and powers. He has shown that He has conquered the ultimate consequence of death itself. All the works of Satan have finally been undone by the Lord Jesus Christ. If we believe in Him, we have been raised with Him. He has 'made us sit together in the heavenly places' with Him (Eph 2:6). We have been raised, we have risen again, we are in Him, we have conquered death and the grave, and we know we shall rise incorruptible and be with Him for all eternity.

In addition to all this, in the light of the Resurrection we know that we can have life anew. He has not only brought life and immortality to light through His Resurrection, He gives us His own life. He took upon Him our human need, He died for our sins, He has taken the guilt away. But more, He has engrafted us into Himself, and He has given unto us—we have received—the divine nature. We have risen with Him as new men and women, a new creation. The works of the devil have thus been destroyed and undone.

But there is more. This work is still being carried on; that is His method. He takes hold of us one by one; He rescues and delivers us out of this world and from Satan one by one. As we believe the message of this gospel, we are translated from the kingdom of darkness into the kingdom of light—the kingdom of God's dear Son. He is building up His own kingdom; he is drawing men and women unto Himself out of the world; He is going on with the work. He is in glory seated at the right hand of God, and He must reign until His enemies shall be made His footstool; He is going on until the number of the elect shall have been gathered in. And when that has happened, He will come again. He will return into this world as King and Lord, and He will finally finish the work. He will come with a mighty sword, and not only evil and sin but Satan himself and all his cohorts shall be cast into the lake of fire and will finally be banished from the sight of God for all eternity. And our guarantee of all this is the glorious fact of the Resurrection: He 'was manifested, that he might destroy the works of the devil.'

Remember then what He has already destroyed, and look forward in anticipation; the blessed hope that faces us as Christian people is that He will destroy these works of the devil utterly, completely and finally; evil and sin will be finally destroyed out of existence, burnt, destroyed for ever. God shall be all and in all, and if we are in the army of the mighty Victor who has already risen from the grave and thereby conquered death, if we belong to Him, we shall behold that final judgment of Satan, and we shall dwell for all eternity in a perfect state with no sin and no sorrow, with no sighing and no tears. There will be no need even for the sun itself, for the light of the glory will be the face of this self-same Lord who was born as a babe in Bethlehem, and we shall bask in that glorious sunshine entirely free from sin for ever and ever. 'The Son of God was manifested'—appeared, came into this world—'that he might destroy the works of the devil.' Thank God for the Victor who came who could conquer even the last enemy, death itself, and give us life which is life indeed.

6

Growing in Grace

Whosoever abideth in him sinneth not: whosoever sinneth hath not seen him, neither known him. Little children, let no man deceive you: he that doeth righteousness is righteous, even as he is righteous. He that committeth sin is of the devil; for the devil sinneth from the beginning. For this purpose the Son of God was manifested, that he might destroy the works of the devil. Whosoever is born of God doth not commit sin; for his seed remaineth in him: and he cannot sin, because he is born of God. In this the children of God are manifest, and the children of the devil: whosoever doeth not righteousness is not of God, neither he that loveth not his brother.

1 JOHN 3:6–10

We have seen that from the end of the second chapter and right through this third chapter, John is showing us that the second great thing we must realise as Christians in this world is that we are children of God. 'Beloved, now are we the sons of God'—not, we are going to be, but we *are*. Now you must hold on to that, says John. You must always retain a firm grasp of it if you want to rejoice while in this world. You are the children of God, and you have a glorious destiny awaiting you.

But, obviously, if you really believe that, you must see that certain things follow of necessity; you cannot claim to be a child of

God and still go on living as if you had not been born again. In other words, one of the first implications of this realisation of our sonship is the realisation of the absolute necessity of living a holy life, and that is the theme of this section from verse 4 to verse 10. We have already looked at this section twice, and I have picked out those two striking statements which are to be found in the fifth and eighth verses. But now we come back to it again, and we shall look in particular at verses 6 and 7, the first part of verse 8 and then verses 9 and 10.

This is notoriously one of the most controversial passages in the New Testament. Of course, no passage in and of itself is controversial, but there has certainly been great controversy over these verses. Anybody who is at all interested in Christian theology, or who has even the faintest interest in doctrine, or indeed anyone who is concerned about living the Christian life, must at some time or another have confronted these statements. The great question which is asked is: do they teach sinless perfection? Do they mean that the Christian in this life can be perfect, delivered altogether from sin not only in act, but also in thought, in desire, in mind, and in every other respect? Anyone who has ever read anything at all on this question of sanctification has at some point come across people who have used these various statements on one side or on the other. So, bearing all that in mind, there are, surely, certain warnings which should be uttered before we attempt to expound a statement such as this one.

First of all, as we look at statements like these, we must try to rid our minds of prejudice. We are all creatures of prejudice; we are born like that as the result of sin, and we tend to start with minds which are biased. One of the most difficult things in life in any realm is to get rid of such prejudice, but surely if we would understand the message of Scripture, we must try to rid our minds of it. Or, to put it another way, we must avoid theories, especially those with respect to sanctification. Again, this is a very difficult thing to do because we all rather like theories; we like to have truth in tabloid form. It seems much easier, it avoids a lot of trouble and mental effort; our natural laziness as the result of sin rather makes us hunger after such easy tabloid thinking, and it is the particular danger in this day and age in which we happen to live. But we must try to avoid theories, and we must try as far as we can to come and look at the Word itself as it is; and above all we must avoid a controversial spirit.

By that I mean that when we come across some of these statements, immediately they become battle cries! Immediately we hear these words, we take sides; we are either going to be for or against sanctification or sinless perfection, and so we become impervious to the message of the Scripture itself. So whenever we come to a passage like this that has so often been discussed in the past, we must make an unusual effort to rid our minds of a mere controversial spirit or a desire to prove that we are right and that somebody else is wrong. Rather, we should have a desire to discover the truth in order that we may apply it in our lives.

If you read the history of the Church you will find that oftentimes, in contending about a passage of Scripture like this, people on both sides have denied the real teaching of the passage. In their desire to prove that they were right they have been guilty of bitterness. Sometimes those who argued for sinless perfection contended in such a way that they proved they were not sinless and indeed not perfect! The spirit of controversy was such that they forgot the truth about which they were arguing and debating. Therefore it is necessary that we should bear this in mind. I suppose the classic discussion of this matter is really to be found in the eighteenth century. I do not want to discuss it historically here, but those who are familiar with the great story of the Evangelical Awakening of that century will remember how there was a very striking cleavage between John Wesley and his followers on the one hand, and the followers of Whitefield and others on the other. There was a great discussion which went on for many decades on this whole question of sinless perfection, and these words which we are considering here were to be found prominently at the heart and centre of the discussions.

Now the great question for us to face is this: Do these statements, which are made here about the Christian, refer to individual, particular acts of sin, or is the Apostle referring to something else? Let me remind you again of some of these statements: 'Whosoever abideth in him sinneth not'—does that mean *particular* acts of sin or does it not? 'Whosoever sinneth hath not seen him, neither known him'—again we must ask the same question. 'He that doeth righteousness is righteous, even as he is righteous,' 'He that committeth sin is of the devil,' 'Whosoever is born of God doth not commit sin'—do those mean individual acts of sin? 'For his seed remaineth in him: and he cannot sin.' Does that mean that a person cannot perform or do individual acts of sin because he or she is born of God? 'In this the children of God are manifest, and the children of the devil; whosoever doeth not righteousness is not of God, neither he that loveth not his brother.' So that is the question we have to face. Are these statements referring to separate, particular acts of sin? If they do, then I think it is perfectly clear that the Apostle is teaching sinless perfection, but the question is, do they mean that?

Let us look at it in this way: First of all, I think we must understand the grammar, and although we are approaching a passage of Scripture, surely the first and the obvious thing to do is to make certain of the exact statement which is before us. We believe that the Word of God is definitely inspired, but that does not mean that every translation is definitely inspired. We must be sure we have understood the true meaning of the Word. So what does the grammar tell us? Well, I think that all the authorities are agreed that all the verbs which are used in this section are present and continuous. In other words, they describe character and prevailing habit rather than particular acts.

Now that applies to all the verbs from verse 4 to verse 10. Verse 4 reads like this: 'Whosoever committeth sin transgresseth also the law: for sin is the transgression of the law.' But a better way of translating that would be: 'Every one who *keeps on doing sin* keeps on breaking the law, or doing lawlessness.' These verbs all carry that meaning of keeping on, so that we render the sixth verse like this: 'Whosoever keeps on doing sin hath not seen him, neither known him.' Therefore when we come to the ninth verse we read: 'The one begotten of God does not *keep on sinning* because God's seed abides in him and he is not able to *keep on sinning*.' So John is talking about those who keep on doing sin, who keep on being guilty of lawlessness, and therefore, on the other side, he says that, 'Whosoever is born of God does not keep on doing sin.' That is the first consideration.

But let me also put this consideration to you: Take, for instance, the full implication of the statement made in verses 6 and 9. We must take the statement as a whole and observe exactly what is stated; and we must also bear in mind the other passages of Scripture and make sure that our exposition of one section of Scripture will never contradict another section.

So take the whole of verse 6 and see the position into which it lands you if you regard John as speaking about individual acts of sin. 'Whosoever abideth in him sinneth not; whosoever sinneth hath not seen him, neither known him.' Now if that means particular acts of sin, then John is saying, 'Whosoever abides in Him does not commit acts of sin; whosoever commits acts of sin has not seen Him nor known Him.' And that means that a person who is guilty of individual acts of sin is not a Christian: 'he hath not seen him, neither known him.' So if you are conscious of having committed acts of sin, then according to this statement, you are not a Christian at all! That is the implication if we say that John here is referring to individual acts of sin.

But consider his words in the ninth verse: 'Whosoever is born of God doth not commit sin; for his seed remaineth in him: and he cannot sin, because he is born of God.' Now if John is referring to individual acts of sin, then he is saying that the man who is born of God, the man who is truly a Christian, does not commit any acts of sin at all; so that, again, if you do commit acts of sin you are not a Christian.

So it is important that we should take the whole statement. What happens generally in discussions about this matter is that people only want one half of the verse. They say, 'Doesn't John say, "Whosoever abideth in him sinneth not"? As long as you abide in Him, you don't commit acts of sin.' But they forget the second part, 'Whosoever sinneth hath not seen him, neither known him.' Then again, they quote the first part of verse 9: 'Whosoever is born of God does not commit sin.' 'There,' they say, 'it is quite plain,' but they forget the statement, 'for his seed remaineth in him: and he cannot sin, because he is born of God.' It seems to me that there, again, is a powerful consideration which must force us to the conclusion that John is not talking about individual acts of sin. He is talking about a state or habit, about people who keep on doing sin.

Or we can put it another way, like this: Take the positive statements of verses 7 and 8–'Little children, let no man deceive you: he that doeth righteousness is righteous, even as he is righteous. He that committeth sin is of the devil; for the devil sinneth from the beginning'; and then the tenth verse, 'In this the children of God are manifest, and the children of the devil: whosoever doeth not righteousness is not of God, neither he that loveth not his brother.' Now I think that the positive statements in those verses are again of vital importance, and we must observe very carefully the way in which the Apostle makes them. You would have imagined that he would have put the statement the other way round–'He that is righteous doeth righteousness,' but John does not put it like that. He says, 'He that doeth righteousness is righteous,' and I think his object is to impress upon our minds the point that what he really is concerned about is our state or condition. He is really comparing people who are righteous with those who are unrighteous, and obviously he does that because he has started the chapter by talking about our being children, referring to our sonship.

So what he is saying is that what really matters is what we *are*. The man or woman who is righteous will show that by living a righteous life; the one who is not righteous shows it by not living a righteous life. That is where his reference to the devil is so significant–'He that committeth sin is of the devil; for the devil sinneth from the beginning.' That is his characteristic, his nature, his habit; that is his way of living. That is the thing that is so true of the devil: he sins from the beginning; he *goes on sinning*. 'And the man,' John says, 'who goes on sinning is, therefore, the man who is proclaiming that he has the kind of nature that the devil has. He does not have the new nature that the Christian has.'

I suggest to you, therefore, that those considerations taken together surely should persuade us that the Apostle is not here considering individual acts of sin at all, because that would be a doctrine of sinless perfection. It would also prove that there was no such thing as a Christian at all, because we have this clear statement that the Christian cannot sin—if he means that. So what the Apostle is dealing with is the general state and prevailing condition.

But perhaps we can reinforce this conclusion by putting certain other considerations also before us. We must remember that the Apostle here is speaking about *all* Christians. Now some of the people who believe in sinless perfection tell us that the Apostle here is only talking about *some* Christians. But at this point they become inconsistent, because they forget the message of verse 6; they say he is only speaking about some, but John is speaking about all Christians: 'Whosoever abideth in him sinneth not.' If a man does not abide in Christ, he is not a Christian at all; to be a Christian means to be abiding in Christ. Now there are some who would have us believe that you can be a Christian without abiding in Christ, but surely that denies the whole doctrine of the rebirth. We are either in Christ or we are not, and if we are not in Christ we are not Christians at all. 'If any man hath not the Spirit of Christ, he is none of his' (Rom 8:9); if we have not been born of the Spirit we are not Christians. You cannot be in Christ one day and out the next; every Christian is in Christ and abides in Him. No, John is not only speaking to certain Christians—he is speaking to all Christians.

Neither is he speaking of some ideal which is set before us or of some object to which we might attain; nor is he speaking only of the new nature that is in us. Let me remind you, there are some who would interpret this statement in that way; they say, 'Whosoever is born of God doth not commit sin,' and when you ask them what that means, they reply that John is talking about the new nature. They say that he is saying that the 'new man' in the Christian cannot sin. But John is not talking about the new man only—he is talking of Christians as they were and as they are; he is talking about us just as we are, as human personalities. He does not say that the new nature of the Christian cannot sin; he says, '*Whosoever is born of God*' cannot sin, and it is I, as a believer, who am born of God; it is the individual who is born again. My new nature is not born again. I have a new nature because I am born again, and the statement is about me and not the new nature. Indeed, there is nothing more dangerous than this, to divide up the personality like that, and it is also a very false piece of psychology just to say that these statements have reference only to the new nature.

So let me try to sum all this up. The Apostle is referring to the general tenor of life of Christian people, and in effect this is what he teaches: If you are truly born of God, if you are a child of God, if the seed of God has entered into you, if you are truly a partaker of the divine nature, then it is bound to affect your life in a profound sense. You will be unlike the man or woman who has not been born again. The characteristic of men and women in their natural state is that they are like the devil; and the characteristic of the evil nature is that they go on sinning, they dwell in sin. The whole atmosphere of that life is one of sin continuing.

But that is not any longer the case with those who have been born again and who have received the divine seed in their nature. They have been made different; they have been lifted out of the realm of sin and have been put into a new realm. They have been taken out of the kingdom of darkness and are now citizens of the kingdom of light; they are people who are walking in the light. That does not mean that they are sinless or perfect; no, but they are walking in the light and not in the darkness. The general condition and appointment of their life, the whole level of their existence, is one of righteousness; they are righteous people, holy people, not perfect people. They are saved, but the fact that they are saved does not mean that they are sinless and absolutely perfect. Yet they are essentially different from the men and women who are still sinners.

That, surely, is the teaching of the apostle at this point. It is the only way in which it can be interpreted which can avoid these contradictions and those false claims that inevitably result if we teach that the Apostle is referring to individual acts of sin. What he says is that he who 'abideth in him' does not keep on committing sin. He tells us that those who abide in Christ do righteousness; they do not go on being guilty of doing that which is wrong. The whole tone and level and attitude of their life has become entirely different, and it is in that sense that it is true to say of them that they literally cannot go on doing sin. Is that not true to experience? The seed of God abides in these people; the new nature that is in them makes it quite impossible.

Let me put it like this: It is the whole question of levels. Those who are not Christians, though they may be morally able to raise their heads, are essentially on a low level. What is the position of Christians? We can put it like this: Their lives are on a different level; they are up on that high level. Alas, they fall into sin occasionally, but they do not stay on the ground–they get back to the high level. They know that they have sinned; they hate sin and repent and confess their sin, and the blood of Jesus Christ again covers them, and back they go walking in the light. It does not mean that they are in a state of sinless perfection, but, thank God, it does mean they know that they are new men and women; they know there is a seed of righteousness in them; they cannot live as they lived before; they have been translated into the kingdom of God's dear Son.

But now when I say something like that, I am quite sure that there are those who want to raise certain objections. 'Are you not implying,' they ask, 'that there is imperfection in God's great plan of salvation? Aren't you there suggesting that God does not deliver us entirely from sin? Aren't you putting a limit on the power of the Lord? Surely,' they say, 'you cannot teach that, because it implies this imperfection!'

Well, my way of answering these objections is to ask some further questions. Why was it that God did not destroy Satan entirely and completely when our Lord was here on the earth? He could have done so; why didn't He? Why is Satan allowed to live and persist and continue? What is the answer to that question? Or let me ask another. Why is it that the moment any person believes on the Lord Jesus Christ as his or her personal Saviour and Redeemer he is not from then onwards entirely delivered from sin and made perfect? God could do it. There is no limit to His power; all things are possible with Him. I put it like that to show that merely to ask such questions is surely an irrelevance, and it is not for us to ask why God does not do this and that. What we must do is to face the facts of experience and the plain teaching of Scripture.

Is it not perfectly clear, therefore, that God in His own wisdom and eternal will has chosen that the plan of salvation shall work out in this way? Satan has been left. The power of sin is not immediately destroyed in us. God has chosen to do this work gradually. This word '*seed*' (v 9)˙ is rather significant. Does that not simply mean God's method and plan in every realm? In the realm of nature you sow the seed, but it may be weeks and months and perhaps years before you get the full bloom. Why does God do it like that? My answer is, I do not know, but that is God's method; it is His way, and it seems to me that is what we are taught in the Scriptures. We are taught about being 'babes in Christ,' we are taught about growing and developing, we are taught about 'growing in grace.' John has already dealt with that when he said, 'Every man that hath this hope in him purifieth himself, even as he is pure' (v 3). It is a process, a development, and surely if we do not interpret a section like this in that way, then it means that we are denying what he has already told us in the first chapter—'If we say we have no sin, we deceive ourselves, and the truth is not in us' (v 8).

John's object in writing is 'that ye sin not. And if any man sin, we have an advocate with the Father . . .' (2:1). But why is that, if the Christian is immediately delivered and made perfect? No, this is a great mystery. It is not for us to understand, but we must face the facts. Is there anyone who would like to claim that he or she is perfect? Well, if you interpret this passage as referring to individual acts of sin, then if you are not perfect, you are not a Christian. No, we must avoid that; we must realise that experience, the experience of the greatest saints, denies this teaching of sinless perfection, and we see that that is not in accordance with the teaching of Scripture.

Lastly, this exhorts us to strive to purify and cleanse ourselves and to interpret Scripture in our daily lives. No, we do not just have to submit and resign ourselves in order to be made perfect; we are to understand the Scriptures and their doctrine. We are to see their implication and to implement them in our daily lives. Is this discouraging? To me it is the height of encouragement, for what I am told is that if I am a Christian at all, if I am a child of God and the divine seed is in me, then God has started to work in me. He will go on, and He will bring it to perfection. But He does so by opening my mind and understanding; He reveals sin to me; He tells me to put these things into practise, to press on and to strive; and He gives the final assurance that if I confess my sin He is faithful and just to forgive my sins and to cleanse me from all unrighteousness (1:9). And experience confirms that. I cannot continue in sin. I cannot live that life of sin; my very new nature objects to it, and I rise out of it. I confess, I acknowledge my sin, I go back, and I strive to walk in the light.

Let us all examine ourselves. Do you find it possible to continue in sin, to keep doing sin? If you do not, it is because you have been born again; the seed of God remains in you, and you cannot go on doing sin because you are a child of God and an heir of eternal bliss. If, therefore, we say that we are the children of God, let us go on to prove it; let us demonstrate it by living that righteous life, even as the Son of God Himself lived it and exemplified it when he was here on earth. 'Every man that hath this hope in him purifieth himself, even as he is pure.'

7

From Death to Life

In this the children of God are manifest, and the children
of the devil: whosoever doeth not righteousness is not of
God, neither he that loveth not his brother. For this is the
message that ye heard from the beginning, that we should
love one another. Not as Cain, who was of that wicked one,
and slew his brother. And wherefore slew he him? Because
his own works were evil, and his brother's righteous.
Marvel not, my brethren, if the world hate you. We know
that we have passed from death unto life, because we love
the brethren. He that loveth not his brother abideth in
death. Whosoever hateth his brother is a murderer: and ye
know that no murderer hath eternal life abiding in him.

1 JOHN 3:10–15

In these verses and in those that follow, we find ourselves facing
the next great appeal and exhortation which this Apostle
addresses to these first Christians in terms of their wonderful
position as children of God. The first point we saw was that if we
are truly the children of God, then we must live a righteous life, and
now here, starting at the end of the tenth verse, John takes up the
second argument under this question of sonship. It is that as children of God we are not only to obey God's laws and live the righteous life, we are also to love one another. The very fact that we are
children in and of itself presupposes this, but because we are so slow

to realise that in practise, the Apostle provides us with certain arguments, and again his logic is surely quite irresistible. Reading these words we are left in the position that this is not a matter to be debated. It is quite inevitable; certain things lead inevitably to certain conclusions, and John is showing us how this question of loving one another as brothers and sisters in Christ is inevitably the outcome of our being children of God.

So we must consider carefully the argument which the apostle provides us. It is not enough merely to *say* that we are children of God; we must give proof of that fact, and John therefore puts it in this manner which is so characteristic of him. We have already seen, as we have worked our way through this epistle, that he almost invariably puts his truth in a double form. It is first and foremost an exhortation, and yet his exhortation is at the same time a test.

Take, for instance, this eleventh verse: 'This is the message that ye heard from the beginning, that we should love one another'; that is the exhortation, and yet he puts it in such a way that it becomes quite plain to us that this question of loving one another is not only a duty, it is also a test, for as he goes on to say, if we do not love one another, we are not children of God. He has already said this in verse 10: 'Whosoever doeth not righteousness is not of God, neither he that loveth not his brother.' The man who does not love his brother is not a child of God; it puts him out of court in exactly the same way as his failure to do righteousness puts him out. Here, then, once more we have this great principle which John goes on repeating chapter after chapter; what we are inevitably expresses itself in our lives. The great thing, therefore, that Christians have to concentrate upon is a full realisation of what they are.

Now we can never be tired of repeating this; the New Testament never calls upon us to do anything without first of all reminding us of who we are. That is its invariable method: doctrine–practise; the whole doctrinal position–the inevitable practical outlook. And John does exactly the same thing here. In other words, he does not ask people to love one another before he has reminded them of the fact that they are children of God. He is right, and therefore he can make his appeal, and that is the New Testament method. It comes to us and says, in effect, 'If you claim to be this, don't you see that it inevitably follows that you ought to behave like that.' There is a kind of inevitable logic in the argument as it is always presented. Mere claims, then, are of no value; it is, rather, our practise that ultimately proclaims what we are.

Now there can be no doubt at all but that John originally wrote this because of certain people in the early church—and there have been people like them ever since—who took the kind of position that nothing matters but our understanding of the truth. This is a position that very often leads to carelessness in practise. It is possible for people to be highly orthodox and yet to be loose in their living. That is what is called *antinomianism*—I am saved, and therefore what I do does not matter at all. And it is the same with this question of brotherly love. There are people who are sometimes so intent upon the cultivation of their own spiritual state that they are lacking in love. They are unconcerned about their brethren; they are so absorbed in their own moods and condition that they forget the practical, obvious duty of the Christian life.

Now John is here showing that that is something which is a self-contradiction; true Christians, being what they are, are people who of necessity must 'love one another.' 'This,' says John, 'is the message—you have heard it from the beginning: we are to love one another'; and you cannot read the New Testament, even in a cursory and superficial manner, without seeing that this is one of the great messages that is impressed upon us and repeated everywhere. If you read especially those tender passages in John's Gospel, from chapters 13 to 17, where our Lord addresses His followers just under the shadow of the cross and gives them His last message, you will find that this is His final appeal. This is the message that He keeps on repeating—'A new commandment I give unto you, that ye love one another' (John 13:34); 'By this shall all men know that ye are my disciples, if ye have love one to another' (v 35). John therefore has a right to say, 'This is the message that ye heard from the beginning,' because our Lord repeated and emphasised it.

Then if you read the various New Testament epistles you will find that it is everywhere. It does not matter who the writer is—they all repeat this message. They never forget the impression that was made upon their minds by those statements of our Lord, so they go on appealing for love. Think of 1 Corinthians 13 and various other notable passages. You must not be jealous and envious of one another, 'rendering evil for evil' (1 Pet 3:9). 'That is the old life,' they say, 'but you are in a new life; so you must love one another.' And this kind of exhortation goes on even beyond the New Testament canon. We know as a literal fact of history that there was nothing that so impressed the ancient world as the way in which Christians loved one another–this great process of demolishing 'the middle wall of partition' (Eph 2:14), the way in which Jews and Gentiles were one in Christ. They showed it in practise, in the way in which they were ready to sacrifice for one another, in the way they shared their goods with one another, and in the way they prayed for one another. These were the things that amazed the ancient world, and they were perhaps more productive in turning people to Christ than anything else. It was said, you remember, 'Behold, how these Christians love one another.' So we are entitled to say that in many ways this is the one great differentiating characteristic of Christian people.

Now we are concerned about this not from a theoretical standpoint, but from an intensely practical one. The argument works in two ways. If we are to experience the full blessing of this Christian salvation, we must love one another; we cannot experience this life without doing it. But I call attention to it not merely from the standpoint of our own personal enjoyment. There is another and greater reason for repeating this exhortation, which is that it is still the way in which the Christian church is going to affect and influence the world. The world in its darkness and blindness still expects something different from the Christian. It expects to see something in the Christian community which no one else can show; so to the extent that we fail to practise and exemplify this great virtue, the whole testimony and witness of the church will be correspondingly weak.

So I want to put this whole question to you in exactly the same way as John does in this section. First of all, he says that if we realise what we are as Christians we will do this. Then, secondly, he says that the proof that we are truly Christians is that we love one another. So let us consider now his first argument. The first thing that is of vital importance, says John, is that we should realise what it means to be a Christian. What is a Christian? What is happening to the Christian? What is it that makes Christians what they are? What is the ground or the basis on which this great superstructure of brotherly love can be erected?

Well, here John tells us three things about the Christian, and I pause at them because they are so wonderful. It does seem to me more and more that what accounts for most of our failures in Christian living is our failure to realise what we are. It is our failure to realise what God has done to us, what has happened to us. Our whole tendency always is to rush to practical applications before we have truly grasped what we are. I have already reminded you that the whole emphasis of the New Testament is put in that way. We must think less and less of doing and more and more of being. If we only are what we ought to be, then the doing will more or less look after itself; and John here reminds us in these wonderful verses of what we are as Christians and what has happened to us.

Let me note these three things. The first we find in verse 14— 'We know that we have passed from death unto life, because we love the brethren.' What then is the Christian? The first thing we are told is that the Christian is someone who has passed from death unto life. What is it that makes Christians primarily different from those who are not Christians? Christians are not just those who go to a place of worship on a Sunday. No, according to the New Testament they are essentially different; they have 'passed from death unto life.'

Now, what does this great conception have to give us? Let me put it like this: According to the teaching of the New Testament everywhere, we all by nature are in a state of spiritual death. I am not only referring to those who are guilty of gross and violent and obvious sins. No, this is true of everybody born into this world. We are born in sin and 'shapen in iniquity'; by nature, by birth we are all 'the children of wrath.' We are born into the realm of death, and we exist in that realm as we are by nature. This is, of course, the result of the Fall; that is the result of man's sin at the beginning. When God made man He said to him, 'If you obey these laws of Mine, you will go on living; if you break them, then you will die.' Man broke God's law and sinned against Him, and he died; and the result, as Paul puts it in Romans 5, is that death reigns. The world has become a world of death, and we are born into a condition in which we are dead–dead spiritually–dead in trespasses and in sins. We are born into the realm of death, and we live in that atmosphere and condition of death.

'From death unto life'–what does this state of death mean? Let me summarise for you what the Bible tells us in various places about this state in which we are by nature. The first thing it means is that we do not know God, that we are outside the life of God and of His Son, Jesus Christ. At the end of His life our Lord said, 'This is life eternal, that they may know thee, the only true God, and Jesus Christ, whom thou hast sent' (John 17:3). So if that is life, then death is the exact opposite. It means not to know God, to be outside the life of God, to have no fellowship with Him, to receive nothing from Him, to be living a life entirely apart from Him.

And that is what the New Testament, and indeed the Bible everywhere, tells us about the state of men and women as they are by nature–they are without life, in death. They do not know God, they have no trafficking or business with Him, and their life is not centred upon Him. To them, God is just some terrible force or power or some philosophical category, or someone to be hated. They are living altogether apart from God. God does not enter into their calculations, and they do not experience anything of the joy that comes from an intimate knowledge of Him. They are, as Paul puts it, 'without God in the world' (Eph 2:12). That is the first thing that characterises this state of death.

But another characteristic, and one which follows of necessity from the first one, is that such people are entirely dead to spiritual things. 'We,' says John, 'have passed from death unto life.' 'You hath he quickened, who were dead in trespasses and sins,' said Paul in writing to the Ephesians (2:1). Those who are dead are dead to the value of their soul; they are quite oblivious of the importance of life in this world and its relationship to their eternal destiny. They do not know why God has given them the gift of life; they are unconcerned about these things. Their interest lies in eating and drinking and enjoying themselves, living for this life and world; and they do not realise that there is within them something which is imperishable. They do not realise that God has made them body, soul, and spirit. They forget the highest category of all; they are living only in the lower realm, utterly dead to spiritual things.

Furthermore, they are not aware of the nature of sin and of evil. They do not realise the terrible spiritual conflict that is going on in this life and world between God and Satan, the powers of heaven and of hell. When you talk to them about sin they laugh at you. They say, 'Surely nobody nowadays believes in sin! That is the old thing that people burdened themselves with a hundred years ago; it is just some kind of imagination that people conjure up out of the past.' They do not understand the nature of the spiritual conflict and the whole position in this world, through which they are rapidly moving to an ultimate end which they cannot avoid. They are spiritually dead; they live to the material and physical, to the seen and temporal, and the unseen and eternal are outside their ken and interest.

Of course the inevitable result of that is that they live a certain type of life, and the type of life that is lived by the person who is thus spiritually dead is perfectly described in Ephesians 2. They walk, says the Apostle there, according to 'the prince of the power of the air'; they are subject to 'the lusts of our flesh, fulfilling the desires of the flesh and of the mind' (vv 2-3). That is it. And is it not obvious in the world in which we find ourselves? Being dead to God and the life and the things of God, men and women live according to these lusts and desires, and it leads to all the miserable, wretched kind of life that you see depicted in the morning newspapers, in the proceedings in the courts, and in all the loudness and clamour and ugliness of life at this moment.

And the last thing we see about such a life is that it is a life which becomes more and more dead as you go on in it. 'The wages of sin is death' (Rom 6:23) and in that life of death, men and women go on dying. That is one of the most terrible things about it. Trace the life stories of those who never become Christians, and you will find a gradual degeneration and decline. In their earlier years, perhaps, they were interested in ideals and idealism, proposing to do certain things. But watch them as they go on. They gradually shed one thing after another; a kind of cirrhosis enters into the soul and imagination, and they go down and down and lose everything that is uplifting and ennobling. There is a kind of hardening process, dying in death, putrefying in a state of sin.

Now that, according to this description which is given here and everywhere else in the Bible, is the state of everybody born into the world by nature, a state of death. 'Thank God,' says the Apostle here, 'that is no longer our position.' To be a Christian means that you pass from death unto life and nothing less than that. Though we were dead in trespasses and in sins, we have been quickened. God in His mercy has looked upon us and by His Spirit has begun to deal with us. He has awakened and aroused us; He has put into us the principles of life, and we are passed from death into another realm altogether. That is what it means to be a Christian—not just deciding to live a better life than you lived before, not just establishing certain moral maxims and principles and making a great effort to keep them. No; it is a change in nature, a *translation*. These are the terms of the New Testament: we have been translated from the kingdom of darkness into the kingdom of His dear Son. Or, as Peter puts it, 'which in time past were not a people, but are now the people of God . . . who hath called you out of darkness into his marvelous light' (1 Pet 2:10-9). It is the same idea, and it is everywhere in the New Testament.

How, then, do we know that we are in this realm of light, the realm of life? Well, this means the exact opposite of everything I have been describing. The people who have passed from death unto life are those who can say that they know God. 'This is life eternal, that they may know thee, the only true God, and Jesus Christ whom thou hast sent' (John 17:3). Do you know God, my friend? This is life eternal; have you life? I am not asking whether you believe certain things; that is possible intellectually. Rather, I am asking, have you life, are you in the realm of life, do you know God, do you know the Lord Jesus Christ? Those who have life do know this, for this is life eternal. When you pray, do you know that you are speaking to God? Is it just a question of dropping on your knees and offering up a number of pious hopes and aspirations, or do you know that God is there? Is there something happening between you and God; are you in real communion with Him?

The only people who know that are those who have life within them. They are no longer dead in trespasses and sins; they have been quickened, born again. They have been given a new life, and they are aware of this life within them. They can say, 'I live; yet not I, but Christ liveth in me' (Gal 2:20). They are aware of certain things in which they were not interested before and to which they paid no attention. They are aware of their own spiritual being and nature; they begin to take an interest in spiritual things. Paul says that those who are Christians are those who '*mind* . . . the things of the Spirit' (Rom 8:5). They take an interest in them; whereas before they were interested only in this world and its affairs, they now become interested in the spiritual kingdom of God. They are concerned about the propagation of the gospel; they pray for the world and its people; they mind spiritual things.

Not only that; they are aware of the fact that there is indeed this principle of life in them. We saw that the others were dying and sinking in death; but these men and women who have been brought from death unto life are aware of growth and development. Life cannot remain static. Look at the flowers; look at the trees during the Spring. Do you not see everything growing and developing? Life must go on; it must develop if you have passed from death unto life. Are you growing in grace; are you developing in the Christian life? Are you further forward than you were a year ago? This life principle must manifest itself.

And perhaps the greatest test of all is that such people desire holiness; they delight in God and in His holy law, and their supreme ambition is to be living this new life with its wondrous principles. They know that God has come to them in His infinite love. I am loath to leave this verse, but we must, so I repeat its message once again: You, beloved Christians, have passed from death unto life; you have been taken out of that grave into which you were born. You are in a new realm; you are new men and women with new principles within you, and you are in a new realm altogether, and you are growing into the likeness of Christ. Do you think of yourself like that? When you think of yourself as a Christian, do you do it in that way? Or is it as just a member of a particular church or denomination, or that you are just a little bit better than somebody else who is a profligate sinner living in the gutters of this world? Do you think of yourself like this: I have passed from death unto life! What a glorious, wonderful thing it is to be a Christian!

But let me just mention the other two things which John tells us here. We have, in a sense, already dealt with the one in the tenth verse. 'In this the children of God are manifest, and the children of the devil: whosoever doeth not righteousness is not of God.' That is it—the second thing that is true of the Christians—that they are *of God*; they are children of God. Christians not only know God, they have received something of God's own nature; they have become 'partakers of the divine nature.' They are born again of the Spirit— that is to say, of God Himself. He has become kin to us, says Paul to the Ephesians; we are members of 'the household of God' (Eph 2:19). So Christians belong to the family of God, and of course they are bound to manifest something of the traits and characteristics of that family life.

Once again, can you fail to be impressed by the fact that you can never make yourself a Christian? You cannot produce the characteristics of God and His family; but if you are a Christian, you do so—you are of God, children of God. Our Lord put this clearly in a verse in the Sermon on the Mount: 'Be ye therefore perfect, even as your Father which is in heaven is perfect' (Matt 5:48). He was talking about the very theme that John is handling in this section: loving people, loving your enemies, doing good to them that hate you, blessing them that use you despitefully and malign you. Do not only love those who love you—anybody can do that; the whole test of your position is that you love your enemies. You who are of God, you who are children of God, you are to reproduce God in your lives.

That is what the Christian is. Christians are new men and women, not just people who are better than anybody else. They are essentially different, they are made on a new pattern, they have a new nature within them, they are of God. Therefore you can turn to them and say, 'Be like God; "Be ye therefore perfect, even as your Father which is in heaven is perfect."'

But let me just mention the third thing which John tells us in this section about the Christian. It is in verse 15: 'Whosoever hateth his brother is a murderer: and ye know that no murderer hath eternal life abiding in him.' But I want to put that in a positive form. The third characteristic of Christian men and women is that they have eternal life abiding in them. I am amazed at times at the fact that I, or anybody else who is a Christian, can remain so silent, can live such a poor, unworthy life. Was I not right when I said at the beginning that the whole trouble with us all is that we do not realise what we are? We insist on thinking about this Christian life as some great height which we have to climb. But before we are asked to do anything, we have been made something; we have eternal life abiding in us, otherwise we are not Christians at all.

John has given us the same idea in verse 9: 'Whosoever is born of God doth not commit sin; for his seed remaineth in him.' The life of the Christian is one which is mastered, governed, controlled by a new principle of life. God is working in the Christian. 'Work out your own salvation,' says Paul, 'for it is God which worketh in you both to will and to do of his good pleasure' (Phil 2:13). That is it—eternal life abiding in us. He has implanted it in us, He has put it into us; it is like a ferment working and developing and influencing, and it is irresistible. Ultimately it is producing a new man or woman, forming us according to the image and pattern of life; this principle of life abides in us and goes on. It is the kind of thing that one sees in the Spring. You notice this about the leaves that were on the trees in the winter. What is it that takes them away? People do not pull them off! No; the new leaf comes and pushes the old leaf off. It is the same here. It is what Thomas Chalmers called 'the expulsive power of the new affection'—eternal life abiding in us.

I cannot do better than put it in verses of Scripture: 'Now unto him that is able to do exceeding abundantly above all that we ask or think, *according to the power that worketh in us* . . .' (Eph 3:20). Or again: 'whom we preach, warning every man, and teaching every man in all wisdom; that we may present every man perfect in Christ Jesus; whereunto I also labour, striving according to his working, which worketh in me mightily' (Col 1:28-29).

So I put it in the form of a question again: are you aware of a mighty power working within you? Do you know there is a new life principle in you? Are you aware of a ferment in your own nature, something pushing you on, urging you forward, making you desire holiness, making you desire to be able to pray in a more worthy manner, longing to know Christ better? Are you aware of something disturbing you; has something been put into you that will not let you remain in that existence of death? We are not Christians unless we know something of that disturbance and turmoil and working within—eternal life abiding in us, going on, moving us and leading us on to other and greater things.

8

The Marks of a Christian

For this is the message that ye heard from the beginning, that we should love one another. Not as Cain, who was of that wicked one, and slew his brother. And wherefore slew he him? Because his own works were evil, and his brother's righteous. Marvel not, my brethren, if the world hate you. We know that we have passed from death unto life, because we love the brethren. He that loveth not his brother abideth in death. Whosoever hateth his brother is a murderer: and ye know that no murderer hath eternal life abiding in him.

1 JOHN 3:11–15

We have begun our consideration of these verses, and we have seen that if we are to experience sonship and its benefit to the full, we must obey God's commandments, we must live as children of God. In a sense, John's argument is that as we are children of God we are therefore like the Lord Jesus Christ; and being like Him, we must live as He lived. He went through this world, which was so cruel to Him, without faltering and without failing because of 'the joy that was set before him' (Heb 12:2). It was that communion and that knowledge which enabled Him, and therefore He always obeyed God. His life was a life full of perfect obedience; as a son He rendered perfect obedience of

95

God's holy will and law. And, secondly, the great characteristic which we see in Him is this quality of love. So John says, 'As you are like Him, you are to display and manifest these things in your daily lives; you are to keep the commandments.' That is the argument up to the middle of the tenth verse, and at the end of that verse he says, 'Whosoever doeth not righteousness is not of God, neither he that loveth not his brother.' He introduces there the theme that is now occupying our attention, and he proceeds to deal with it from verse 11 well on towards the end of this particular chapter.

Now the Apostle's method is one which is full of interest. It is his statement that if we are children of God and realise what that means, then we must of necessity be like the Lord Jesus Christ in our conduct. And the point that I want to make is that this is not so much an argument which John deduces, as a statement of something which is absolutely inevitable. John is not asking us here to deduce certain things from our position of sonship. He says, 'If you are God's children, then you must do so-and-so, and if you do not, you are not His children.' It is the inevitability that I wish to emphasise. This is his argument with regard to this question of loving one another, exactly as it was with regard to conduct. He says, 'Whosoever is born of God doth not commit sin; for his seed remaineth in him: and he cannot sin, because he is born of God' (v 9). We have already looked at that, and it is just the same with this question of sonship.

In other words, we must again point out that John puts his whole exhortation to us, that we should love one another, in terms of our position. It cannot be said too frequently that the New Testament never asks us to do anything without first of all reminding us of who we are. It does so because its doctrine is that we cannot do the things we are asked to do unless we are children of God. Therefore, let me remind you that the New Testament has no general indication to the world as to how it shall live. Its only message to the world is to repent and believe on the Lord Jesus Christ. But it has a great deal to say to the believer. It starts with our position and then it says, 'Because you are what you are, does it not inevitably follow that you must produce these works?'

We have considered the description that is given of us. There are three things: Christians are those who have 'passed from death unto life'; secondly, they are 'of God'; and lastly, they have eternal life abiding in them. 'Therefore,' says John, 'the vital question you have to ask yourself is this: are you such a person? Can you say that you have passed from death unto life? Do you know that you are of God? Do you know that there is eternal life abiding in you; is that your claim? That should be the claim of every Christian and nothing less. Now,' says John, 'there is, in a sense, no need for you to make a statement about it. What you are will demonstrate very clearly whether there is any substance in your claim or not. You life will prove and demonstrate whether you really are a child of God or whether you are not.'

There is something glorious and yet terrible about the Christian position. We are all the time proclaiming what we are; the world in a sense is right when it tells us that it is more interested in our life than in our statements. Let us never forget that as Christian people, we are the whole time proclaiming what we are. We are bound to. It is inevitable—that is the whole argument at this point. Life and nature simply cannot be hidden. What we are, we are bound to express. It does not matter what our clothing or our disguise may be. Life or nature will show; or as it is sometimes put, 'breeding will out.' The blood that is in us will show itself; we cannot help it. We may even try to conceal it, but it will be there.

Our Lord Himself put this perfectly in the Sermon on the Mount when he said, 'Ye shall know them by their fruits. Do men gather grapes of thorns, or figs of thistles? Even so every good tree bringeth forth good fruit; but a corrupt tree bringeth forth evil fruit. A good tree cannot bring forth evil fruit, neither can a corrupt tree bring forth good fruit' (Matt 7:16-19). It is not a matter to be argued about; people may try to talk as Christians, but they show very clearly in their lives whether they are Christians or not. These are absolutes, and this is precisely the argument of the Apostle at this particular point.

Let us be quite clear about this—the doctrine is not that we make ourselves Christian by loving the brethren and so on. No, rather it is the other way round—that we prove we are Christians by loving the brethren. That is why it seems to me always to be so utterly fatuous and ridiculous to say that there is conflict between the doctrine of James and that of the Apostle Paul. That is the very thing that James said: 'Show me thy faith without thy works, and I will show thee my faith by my works . . . faith without works is dead' (Jas 2:18, 20). It is this very doctrine, the doctrine of this chapter, the doctrine, as we have seen, of the Sermon on the Mount, the doctrine to be found everywhere throughout the New Testament.

Let me put it like this: We have said that what we are and what we claim to be can be checked and proved by our conduct and by our behaviour. 'Very well,' says someone, 'if it is as inevitable as that, what is the point of John's exhorting these people to love the brethren?' There are many answers to that question. One is that while John wants to remind us of our nature and of the life within us, he also wants to encourage us to live life in conformity with that nature, and he also wants to increase our joy by stimulating us to produce still more fruit.

It is, if you like, similar to this: You see a tree bearing fruit, but if you dig round the roots and feed it, you will help to bring forth more fruit. John is just aiding and assisting and stimulating these people. It is exactly the same as when we exhort the child to behave himself and remind him that the whole dignity of the family is in his hands; it is a good thing to remind him what he is in order that he may represent the family in a still better manner.

As Christian people, we should make the claim that we have 'passed from death unto life' and that we are 'of God' and that we have 'eternal life abiding' in us. 'Now,' says John, 'there are absolute proofs of whether this claim of ours is true or not. Here is the first: if we want to know for certain that we are children of God, and therefore Christians, then here is the first test—we have become unlike the world.' That is the first argument in verse 12: 'Not as Cain.' John always starts with the negative—'*Not as Cain*, who was of that wicked one, and slew his brother. And wherefore slew he him? Because his own works were evil, and his brother's righteous.' Cain stands once and for ever in the Bible as the type of the worldly person, the person who is not of God, the unspiritual person; therefore everything that is true of the world, in contradistinction to the Christian, is to be seen in Cain.

What are the characteristics of this worldly type? The answer is that such people are the exact opposite of the Christian. The Christian, as we have seen, is of God, and what we are told about the worldly man here is that he is of the devil—'of that wicked one.'

The second thing we are told about him in verse 14 is that he 'abideth in death,' while the Christian has 'passed from death unto life' and has 'eternal life abiding in him.'

And the third thing, going along with the second, about this worldly man is that he does not have 'eternal life abiding in him'; that is the statement of verse 15. So there is a general description of the worldly person. He is of the wicked one; he belongs to the devil, Satan. He is of the kingdom of darkness, under the tyranny and dominion and thraldom of the god of this world. That is the realm in which he lives; that is the person to whom he belongs. As we have seen, Christ said to such people, 'Ye are of your father the devil' (John 8:44). That is it. And they abide in death. They have not been quickened; the Holy Spirit has not given them life. They are still dead in trespasses and sins, and the awful thing is that they have no principle of eternal life abiding in them.

But let us work this out a little more in particular, for that is only a general description. What in particular do we find to be the characteristics of this life? They are seen clearly in the devil himself and in the kind of life that belongs to him. The great characteristic of such a life is that it is self-centred, a life of self-will and of selfishness. That is what produced the original fall of Satan. He was a perfect being created by God, so why did he fall? It was because he became self-centred. He was not content with spending his eternity in worshipping and glorifying God. He began to think of himself, and he began to feel that he was worthy of more attention. He wanted to live life in his own way and in selfishness, and that is the characteristic of this kind of life. It is an ugly, foul, hateful thing, but you see how it is the great thing in life today—the sheer selfishness of it all, people living for themselves.

And of course the other characteristic is that it is a life of hatred of God and a hatred of good. 'Wherefore,' asks John, referring to

Cain and Abel, 'slew he him? Because his own works were evil, and his brother's righteous.' And that, also, is the second great characteristic of the devil. He hated God, he hated the power and the glory of God, and he turned against all that; and everyone who belongs to the devil does the same thing. The Apostle Paul says, 'The carnal mind is enmity against God: for it is not subject to the law of God, neither indeed can be' (Rom 8:7). 'Ah, but,' we say, 'surely that is not true of good people who are not Christians; there are so many nice people.' But however nice they may be, the carnal mind is enmity against God, it is of the devil, it is of the wicked one, and it manifests itself in some shape or form.

The results of these wrong attitudes are seen clearly in the case of Cain. This evil life of hatred of God and of His holy law, this self-centred, self-willed, selfish life, always is a perverted and an unnatural life, and you see what it did in Cain. Here are two brothers, Cain and Abel, and you see what sin does to a man. A brother should love a brother, but Cain became jealous of his brother, and he hated him to such an extent that he killed him. What made him do it? The two brothers took offerings to God, and God praised the offering of Abel, but He did not praise the offering of Cain, and that made Cain so angry with his brother that he killed him. This is the self-centred life. 'I am so desirous of praise—what is my brother when I am being hated!'

And that is the spirit that rules the world today. That is what produces the horrors of the law courts; that is what produces wars between nations. It is men and women in their self-centredness hating anyone who seems to have something that they have not. Murder is but the logical conclusion of all this. But this is the principle that is in all who are not Christians. Paul has given us a terrible description of this in writing to Titus, 'For we ourselves also were sometime [that is, before we became Christians] foolish, disobedient, deceived, serving divers lusts and pleasures, living in malice and envy, hateful, and hating one another' (3:3).

That is the life of the world. I need not press it; is it not true? Listen to people's conversations. You do not know them, but listen to them as they are talking about somebody else. Listen to the spite and the malice and the envy. Look at their eyes; there is murder in them. They may not actually commit murder, but the principle is there. I am not condemning such poor people; I am sorry for them. Look at the faces of the people who are always criticising somebody else. Look at them; they cannot see themselves. That is the tragedy. If only they saw the ugliness and the venom! Pray for them; have pity on them; they are of the devil, and they are living in malice, hating and hateful. What a terrible, horrible life that is.

Are we like that? It does not need any argument. It is impossible that we have the divine nature abiding in us if we are like that. What we are is proclaimed by what we do and how we behave, and the thing that is essentially and obviously true of Christians is that they are not like the world, 'not as Cain.' They do not have this hateful, horrid spirit in them of jealousy and envy and malice, hating and criticising. Oh, the ugliness! Thank God for the passing from death unto life, from such a world into the kingdom of light, the kingdom of love, the kingdom of God!

The second proof that we are Christians is that the world hates us. Verse 13 says, 'Marvel not, my brethren, if the world hate you.' Again, we do not need any proof; this is absolutely inevitable in view of the first proposition—it is bound to happen. As John puts it here, do not be surprised if the world hates you. It is not surprising in view of what we have been saying.

Let me put this as an historical fact. This is one of the great principles which we find in the Bible from the beginning. There are many people who are in difficulty about this verse. If this is true of you, then you have somehow failed to understand the first great essential divisions of the Bible. The difference between Cain and Abel was in Cain, not Abel. Cain (the world) hates Abel (the Christian). Look at Joseph and his brethren. Look at David and Saul; read the story of how King Saul treated David and tried to get rid of him—the jealousy, envy and malice. Look at the treatment that was meted out to the prophets, those men of God who were trying to save the nation. It is there everywhere.

Look at the supreme example of our Lord Himself. Here is the Son of God incarnate; here is the eternal life in the flesh. Look at the world sneering at Him, how they picked up stones to cast at Him, how they shouted, 'Crucify Him, away with Him!' The world crucified the very Son of God who had come to save it! 'Marvel not, my friends, if the world hate you.' The world does not hate you because you are hateful people; the case of Cain and Abel proves that. Cain did not hate his brother because there was something hateful about him. There was nothing to be hated in Abel, but Cain hated him in spite of that.

Neither does the world hate us because we are good. Let us be quite clear about that. The world does not hate *good* people; the world only hates *Christian* people; that is the subtle, vital distinction. If you are just a good person, the world, far from hating you, will admire you; it will cheer you. And what is true of the individual is true of the whole Church. The psychological explanation is quite simple. The world likes good people because it feels that they are a compliment to itself. So the world applauds them. But the world, we are told, hates Christians, not because they are hateful, not because they are good, not because they do good, but specifically because they are Christians, because they are of God, because they have Christ within them.

I think this does not need any demonstration. If anyone did good in this world, it was the Lord Jesus Christ; but as I have shown you, the world hated Him. It is not goodness—it is this specific thing that makes us Christian that does it. Now I believe that this is one of the most profound and thorough proofs of the new life within us that we can ever have. Our Lord put it like this: 'Think not that I am come to bring peace on earth: I came not to send peace, but a sword. For I am come to set a man at variance against his father, and the daughter against her mother, and the daughter-in-law against her mother-in-law. And a man's foes shall be they of his own household' (Matt 10:34-36). Our Lord has prophesied and predicted this very thing.

Now being good does not divide families. Here is something, and the only thing, that should upset the family relationship. The family will not hate you if you are good and do good. The family will not even hate you if you do wrong; it will forgive things in you that it would not forgive in anybody else—it always has a soft spot for the prodigal son. But become a Christian and live like the Lord Jesus Christ and 'a man's foes shall be they of his own household.'

This is an amazing thing, but this is where the true perversion of sin begins to emerge.

What is the explanation? Well, I think it is quite simple if you read your Bible. To be born again means that you become essentially different from what you were, and you no longer belong to the family as you did before. I can best put this to you by way of an illustration. I knew a man and his wife, indeed I had the pleasure of taking the service when they got married–two highly respectable, moral people. At first they lived a happy married life together. Then the husband was converted and became a Christian. His entire life became different, especially when he began to know this great fondness for the things of God. He attended all the meetings of the church, weeknights as well as Sundays, and he lived for these. On one occasion when he went home from a meeting in the church, his wife (I repeat, a very good, respectable, nice woman, even a member of the church) received him with this greeting: 'I had sooner see you carried helplessly drunk into the house than see you perpetually coming home from these prayer meetings!' She would sooner see him helplessly drunk! Why? Because she had the feeling that he now belonged to someone else; Christ came even before her.[1]

Christ demands that. He said, 'If any man come to me, and hate not his father, and mother, and wife, and children, and brethren, and sisters, yea, and his own life also, he cannot be my disciple' (Luke 14:26). And, you see, the world thus pays tribute to the fact that we are born again and have become children of God. It realises that we have been taken out of the realm of the world and we are in a new family. We cannot enjoy the things it enjoys, and it is offended by this. It says, 'This thing has taken him from me, and I hate it.' Sin does not divide in that sense. The only thing that divides in the very depths is the gospel of Jesus Christ, the new life. But this divides absolutely, and soon a Cain murders even his own brother.

The world hates us because it does not understand us or the life we have. It does not share this life with us, and it feels we are condemning it, even though we may not say a word. But because we are so different, it feels condemned. It feels lost, and it hates the feeling of condemnation, so it hates us. That was why the world hated our Lord. He never did any wrong, He was without sin, He preached that perfect message, He went about doing good, and yet they snarled at Him, the Pharisees especially. This was because by just being what He was, He condemned them. He showed them that He belonged to a different order, a different realm. He was God in the flesh, and everyone who reproduces this will get the same response and reaction from the world. Make sure, my friends, that you are not just good. Make sure you are Christians.

The final proof of the fact that we are Christians is positive—we love the brethren. We are unlike the world, we are hated by it, but verse 14 tells us, 'We know that we have passed from death unto life, because we love the brethren.' It is the final proof, the glorious proof, the positive proof, something again which is quite inevitable; and what John is saying is that we now love Christians as Christians and because they are Christians. Is this not inevitable? Our new nature is one of love; that is what we have been given by the Holy Spirit—the fruit of the Spirit is love. So, having this new nature, there is the principle of life in us which was never there before. It is natural to love members of the family; the world has become unnatural in sin and does not do that, but this is natural, to love members of the family, to love those that are in it as we are.

But the real explanation is that we love the brethren because they are 'of God.' We see God in them, Christ in them; it is the expression of our love to God. As our Lord put it, they share the life of God, which being interpreted is this: if you love God like that, you are bound to love your neighbour as yourself; it is an expression of your love for God.

Let me put it practically, like this: Christians rejoice in the work of God in themselves, and they rejoice to see the same thing in others. So when we see people who have been born again, we want to praise God. We love them because they are in the hands of God, because they are God's workmanship, because we detect this principle of Christlikeness in them. We love them; we rejoice with them in that they also have what we ourselves have got.

But not only that—we love the brethren because we share the same interests; we have been brought out of darkness into light, separated from the world into this new kingdom. We are sharing and are interested in the same thing, in this glorious Word, in this praise of God. We have the same enjoyments as we go through this world of time. And back and beyond it all, we are facing the same destination. We are making for the same glory, we are travellers together through this weary pilgrimage, and we look forward to the glorious day that is coming. We know that our eternity is to be spent together there, beyond time, beyond death. There in the everlasting and eternal glory we are going to bask together in the sunshine of His wondrous peace and all His glory and His grace.

Is it not inevitable that we love one another? We are marching together to Zion; we are going together to the Promised Land. 'Brother clasps the hand of brother,' through being the same in nature, the same in outlook, the same in desires, the same in interests, having the same blessed hope, and seeing the same work in us all. It is not a matter of argument or of deduction; it is something that is absolutely inevitable–'We know that we have passed from death unto life, because we love the brethren.' There are certain people we now love whom we would not love if we were not Christians; as natural people we would not love them, but we now see them in a different way, and we love that in them–we love the brethren.

God grant that as we examine ourselves in the light of these things, we may be able to say together and individually, 'I know that I have passed from death unto life.'

9

Love in Action

Hereby perceive we the love of God, because he laid down his life for us: and we ought to lay down our lives for the brethren. But whoso hath this world's good, and seeth his brother have need, and shutteth up his bowels of compassion from him, how dwelleth the love of God in him? My little children, let us not love in word, neither in tongue; but in deed and in truth.

1 JOHN 3:16–18

We come here, obviously, to the practical side and to the application of what John has already been telling us about 'lov[ing] the brethren.' He has been talking about this love, but, wise teacher and pastor as he is, now an old man who has had a long experience, he realises that you cannot just live these things as general statements, so he comes right down to the practical level. He gives us illustrations in order that we may be perfectly clear in our minds as to what he means, and in order that we may not be deceiving ourselves, because, as he goes on to tell us from verse 19 onwards, this is a matter which is of the most vital importance from the standpoint of Christian experience. It affects our whole condition as we go to God in prayer and our whole thought about ultimately meeting God in the judgment. So it is intensely important from our own personal standpoint and well-being, as well as from the greater standpoint of the testimony and the witness of Christian people in a gainsaying world.

So John comes down to practicalities, and of course in doing this he is doing something that is very characteristic of the New Testament, indeed of the whole Bible. It always becomes practical, it never leaves us a loophole, and that is why we are always without excuse if we do not live this Christian life as we ought. It comes down to details, details which we feel at times to be almost ridiculous, but the Bible knows us so well and it recognises that nothing can be taken for granted. You have to come down to the smallest detail, and John gives us a perfect example of that in these three verses. It takes us from the heights where we have considered the death of Christ on the cross, to humdrum details—the matter of either giving or not giving to a brother in need. We are brought right down to that practical level, and John tells us why he does so.

Now as we address ourselves to the practical aspect of loving the brethren, there is one preliminary point which I feel constrained to make because I believe that there is often a good deal of confusion in people's minds with regard to this question of loving, and I think the confusion can be put most conveniently like this: There are many people who are troubled about this matter and who rather feel in the light of that great statement in verse 14—'we know that we have passed from death unto life, because we love the brethren'— that they are not Christians at all. They confess that they cannot honestly say that they like certain Christian people, and therefore they ask in the light of that text, 'Am I a Christian at all? If I am quite honest, I have to admit that I do not like certain people, and yet I am told that if I do not love the brethren, then I am not a Christian.'

Now I think that the point here is that we have to be careful to draw the distinction between loving and liking, and this is by no means an artificial distinction. It is a very vital one which I could illustrate at great length from the Bible itself. So let me put it at once like this: we are not called to *like* the brethren, but we are called and commanded to *love* them. Furthermore, I would assert that loving and liking are not degrees of the same thing but are essentially different. What is liking? What is it to like a person?

Well, I would say that liking is something natural, something instinctive or elemental, something that is not the result of effort; you find yourself liking or not liking. In other words, liking is something physical and unintelligible.

Now do not misunderstand that. When I say that something is unintelligible, I mean that it does not happen as the result of the operation and the use of the intelligence. Liking is something that belongs to the animal part of life and nature. You find it in the animal world itself; there is something instinctive, something that is just an expression of nature, and it is not intelligent in the sense that it can give reasons for its like or dislike. Or, to put it further, the state of liking is one in which we are naturally interested in the person as such. It is certain qualities of that person, certain things about them which we like or dislike. In other words, liking does not penetrate to the central height of personality; it is an interest in superficial things, appearance, colour, temperament, behaviour or certain mannerisms. Indeed it is something still more physical—almost, we might say, some kind of physical emanation that goes from one to another. If you think of it in terms of the animal kingdom, I think you will see very clearly what I am trying to convey.

But loving is something entirely different. Loving is something which we must think of in terms of God. Now when I talk about love, I obviously do so in the way in which the Bible talks about it, and not in the way in which modern books and articles think about it, which is generally infatuation or some intense form of liking rather than true loving. We will agree, I am sure, that one of the real tragedies of the age in which we live is that this great word has become so debased and misused. I am talking about love, not about infatuation. Love is that which we must always think of in terms of God, because we are told that 'God is love' (1 John 4:8), and that is the thing about love, as John proceeds to tell us in these three verses.

Therefore, we can give this kind of preliminary definition: love is always highly intelligent; nature is not the greatest thing in love; the intellectual and intelligent aspects are indeed the most prominent. Love is never elemental or instinctive, because love is something that penetrates to the person; it goes beyond the superficial and the visible, the carnal and physical attraction, to something bigger and deeper. Indeed, it is an essential part of love that it goes out of its way to do that. Love overcomes obstacles and excuses; it sees beyond what it does not like and minimises it, in order to see the person who is at the back of it.

Now all this inevitably becomes a part of our definition of love, otherwise it would be impossible for God to love the sinner. We draw a distinction often, and we say God loves the sinner in spite of his sin. Love penetrates beyond the ugliness and the unattractiveness; it seeks out something. It is highly intelligent, it is thoughtful, and it is understanding. It is discriminating, and that is why I thus emphasised and stressed the intelligent aspect of love.

Therefore, we can arrive at a further definition: To love those whom we do not like means that we treat them as if we did like them—to choose to act kindly toward them even though we do not like them. Now I trust that will help those who are in difficulty about this matter. The Bible does not ask us to like the brethren, it asks us to love them, and that means, therefore, something like this: From the animal standpoint—and men and women have an animal part of their nature, let us never forget it—we may not like certain Christians. I mean by that, there is none of this instinctive, elemental attraction; they are not the people whom we naturally like; yet what we are told is that to love them means that we treat them exactly as if we did like them.

Now the men and women of the world do not do that; if they do not like people, they treat them accordingly and have nothing to do with them. But Christian love means that we look beyond that. We see the Christian in them, the brother or sister, and we even go beyond what we do not like, and we help that person. Love your brethren—that is the exhortation with which we are concerned.

Having dealt with that preliminary, practical point, let me now go on to call attention more directly to the points which John himself emphasises and stresses in these three verses. But before we consider them in detail, I must point out that it is generally agreed that in verse 16 the words 'of God' should not be there; so the verse should run: 'Hereby perceive we love' or 'Hereby know we love, because he laid down his life for us. . . .'

So then as we come to consider the verses, I shall vary the order in which John puts them, and my only reason for that is that I think it will enable us to end with the grand appeal. John's exhortation, in a sense, is that which is found in verse 18: 'My little children, let us not love in word, neither in tongue; but in deed and in truth.'

Now here we have first of all the danger of being theoretical only. I do not think we need stay long with this; we must all surely know this dangerous possibility in our own lives and experience. What an easy thing it is, not only in this matter of love, but in the whole question of practising and living the Christian life, how easy it is to be content only with thoughts and with feelings and with expressions of what we believe and feel, and to fail utterly and entirely to put it into practise. How easy it is to fall in love with loving instead of actually loving! How easy it is, when we are alone in our room, perhaps reading a wonderful book about love and about the actions of some great saint, how we seem to be thrilled and captivated and lifted up as it were into the heaven of heavens. We say, 'Thank God for this,' and then the next minute we go out and we are annoyed or bad-tempered or we fail in some simple elementary duty.

We all know about this. How easy it is to be in love with love; how easy it is to be content with elevating thoughts, to feel on Sunday, in church, that having contemplated the love of God in Christ, we can go back into the world and be absolutely different. Then something annoys us in the church porch or on the street and, almost before we have left the place, suddenly we go down and fail. Now that is what John is concerned about. 'My little children, let us not love in word, neither in tongue; but in deed and in truth.'

John is very concerned about this because, as he goes on to show, misbehavior here is a denial of God. There is a sense in which you cannot love in word and in thought only, as I am going to show you. So this is the danger which we must constantly keep in mind, and I wonder whether it would not be true to say that this is perhaps a greater danger with regard to the whole matter of love and love for one another than it is with regard to any other aspect of the Christian life and practise.

I suppose that this is so because 'the greatest of these is charity

[love]' (1 Cor 13:13); love is, as it were, the ultimate, because of its very nature and delicacy. I do not know whether my experience has been yours, but I do find that this is one of the more difficult things—and not only for myself; I am referring especially to my experience with others. I think it is the simple, honest truth for me to say that the two most difficult men with whom I have ever had to cooperate were two men who were concerned about the question of pacifism. I remember one of these two brethren making a most impassioned statement with regard to it; he was one of those people who would die for their pacifist principles, and he was delivering an address on loving our enemies. After I had listened to him, I was constrained to point out in the discussion later on that some of us might have to remember that before we talk about loving our enemies, we may have to start with loving our brethren! It is possible for us to say and to talk a great deal about these things and yet to be jealous and envious of one another and to be harsh and critical of one another.

This is one of the paradoxes of love. I would say that people who emphasise love for others in their teaching are those who of all others must watch that they are not bitter in their spirit. They may be more bitter in their spirit than those who are not pacifists, because that is the central thing on which they concentrate. Now that is the point which John is making; the more we consider this question of love, the more careful have we to be that we are not just in love with an idea and utterly fail to put it into practise. I think that the ultimate explanation is probably that if we set ourselves up, especially as exemplars of this question of loving the brethren, then we can be sure that the devil will make a special target of us. It is in the greatest meeting that we have to be most careful; it is when we have been unusually drawn out in prayer, whether in private or in public, that we have to watch ourselves. It is when we talk about our faith to others, it is when we are nearest to God ourselves, that the devil will be most active. It was after the baptism and when the Holy Ghost descended upon Him in the Jordan in the form of a dove that our Lord was led into the wilderness to be tempted of the devil.

Let us, therefore, bear that general point in mind; but we must enforce it by some of the solemn warnings about it which are to be found in the New Testament. Let me mention some of them. Take, for instance, what our Lord says towards the end of the Sermon on the Mount. He talks about those people who will say, 'Lord, Lord, haven't we done this, that and the other because of our love for You?,' and He will say to them, 'I never knew you: depart from me, ye that work iniquity' (Matt 7:23). He goes on to say that there is no point in saying, 'Lord, Lord,' unless you do His commandments, and then He ends it all with the terrible picture of the two houses— the house built on the rock and the house built upon the sand. He portrays the man who hears our Lord's sayings and does them as being controlled by them and lifted up by them; he is the man who builds his house upon a rock, a house which stands in the storm and in the flood. But the other man, hearing these sayings of our Lord, says, 'It is marvellous, it is wonderful!' He is moved, but he does not do them; he is like the man who builds his house upon the sand. This is no good, and it does not stand in the storm. No; the doing, says our Lord, is absolutely vital and essential.

And then think of the same point as He makes it in the three pictures in Matthew 25. The first is that of the ten virgins, five of whom were wise and five foolish, the latter being the people who did not make sure and who did not take a supply of oil. Then take the parable of the talents and the man who hid his talent in the ground. He did not use it, he did not do what he was told to do. And then lastly comes the picture at the end—the great judgment of the sheep and the goats. Those who are compared to the goats are condemned—what was the matter with them? The trouble with them was that they had not put this supposed love of theirs into practise in the matter of helping one of the 'least of these my brethren.' 'I was in trouble and in prison,' said our Lord, 'and you did nothing for Me.' 'But,' they said, 'Master, when did we either see You in prison or without food or naked, and when did we fail to do these things?' Our Lord's reply is, 'Inasmuch as ye did it not to one of the least of these, ye did it not to me' (Matt 25:45). There, you see, is this same solemn warning about being content only with some vague, general feeling of love and with some precepts which we do not put into practise. Here, surely, is one of the greatest dangers concerning ourselves.

Now perhaps there are those who are in difficulty at this point because of a misunderstanding of the New Testament teaching with regard to this whole matter. The very Scriptures which I have been quoting seem to some to suggest an apparent contradiction. They say, 'We read our New Testament, and we really are confused, because it seems at one time to emphasise the spirit only, then the next time it is pressing the actions only. Which is it?' And they spend their whole time in oscillating between one and the other.

Let me illustrate what I mean. Take for instance 1 Corinthians 13. There the great emphasis is all the time upon the spirit— 'Though I speak with the tongues of men and of angels, and have not charity, I am become as sounding brass, or a tinkling cymbal.' Here is the man who may give his body to be burned, and yet if he has not love, it is of no avail whatsoever. Here is a man constantly doing things, putting it into practise, giving his goods to the poor, a wonderful man in action, and yet we are told that this is utterly useless because his spirit and motive are wrong.

But then there is another side to this that seems to put all its emphasis upon the action. We saw in Matthew 7 that our Lord, in talking about the response to His sayings, spoke about the man who '*doeth them not*'; and that is the thing that condemns; it is the doing that matters. Consider also His parable about the two sons in Matthew 21, how the father went to one of his sons and said, 'Son, go work today in my vineyard. He answered and said, I will not; but afterward he repented, and went. And he came to the second, and said likewise. And he answered and said, I go, sir; and went not. Whether of them twain,' asks our Lord, 'did the will of his father? They say unto him, The first' (vv 28-31), and that is absolutely right. There again the emphasis is not on saying to your father, 'Yes, father, I will go and work in the vineyard.' 'The question is,' says our Lord, 'will you *go and work* in the vineyard'; the whole emphasis is on the doing.

And you remember, too, our Lord's solemn words just before the end as they are recorded in John 14:21-24. Let me pick out the salient words: 'He that hath my commandments, *and keepeth them*, he it is that loveth me; . . . if a man love me, he will keep my words. . . . He that loveth me not keepeth not my sayings.' 'That is the test,' says our Lord. It is not the people who spend hours before the cross or before a picture or who spend their time in some mystical state. Love must not be thought of in that way: 'He that keepeth my commandments, he it is that loveth me'—that is the way.

Well, what is the explanation of the apparent contradiction? It is to be found in the nature of love. I feel that all our troubles arise because of our loose and sentimental thoughts about love. The nature of love is surely shown us perfectly in Luke 7, in the story of what happened in the house of the Pharisee who invited our Lord in for a meal. When our Lord was seated at the table, an immoral woman came in and fell at his feet; weeping, she washed his feet with tears and wiped them with the hairs of her head and anointed them with ointment. And then you remember what the Pharisee thought, and the surprise of the other people. And what our Lord said to them all in effect was this: 'Simon, love is something which by its nature always expresses itself. Love is something which by its very nature has got to go into action. This woman loves Me, and she shows it by washing My feet and drying them and anointing them with ointment.' Love is always active; if there is no expression, there is no love.

There is another illustration of the same thing in our Lord's teaching in Matthew 18, where He talks about that servant who had been forgiven by his lord and then refused to forgive one of his own servants. Our Lord said, 'Unless you forgive, you will not be forgiven' (Matt 18:23-35).

'Well, doesn't that teach that we merit salvation?' asks someone. 'Doesn't that say that if I can forgive I shall be forgiven?' Nothing of the sort! What it teaches is that the men and women who truly believe and know that they are forgiven by God as the result of God's infinite grace are the people who have the love of God in their hearts, and that love is bound to show itself. Unforgiving people have not been forgiven themselves; those who are forgiven are so broken by it that they cannot but forgive others. They are children of God, and they act like God. In other words the New Testament does not merely exhort us to do things;

it does not merely tell us to obey the rules. Rather, what the New
Testament does is to ask us a question: 'Are you sure that the love
of God is in you?' Or, as an exhortation it says, 'Make sure that the
love of God is in you; and the way to know whether it is in you or
not is this: if it is in you, you will love your brethren.'

Now this is the very nature of love. It must express itself; it is
always active; and if our love does not do that, I say it is not true
love. You see, the real trouble with the person who is seated there
in his study reading beautiful poems or books about love and who
feels that he is controlled by it and that he is a fine Christian is this:
What is really happening to that person is that he is simply in love
with himself, because he appreciates these elevating thoughts. He
is loving himself because he thinks he is in love. He has turned in
upon himself, and that is the very antithesis to love; love does not
look at itself—it is absorbed in the object of its love.

However, we need not remain in mere theory. John brings us
right down to the practical level. He gives us an abundant illustration in the case of this man who shuts up his 'bowels of compassion'—who has no pity. Here is a man who has received this world's
goods; then he sees a brother in Christ who is in need, and he has
no pity on him. He does not do anything about it, and he goes on
as if he had not seen it. Now there is no need to argue; there is no
love of God in that man, because he is thinking only of himself. 'He
may be thinking beautiful thoughts about the love of God, but it is
valueless,' says John. 'If he had the love of God in him, he would
have to do something about it.'

But finally John puts it in the positive form of the royal pattern,
the royal example: 'Hereby we know the love of God, *because he laid
down his life for us.*' The great commentary on this is to be found in
the second chapter of Paul's epistle to the Philippians. What was
the characteristic of that perfect life? Here are headings. He saw our
predicament, and He had compassion. There in the bosom of God,
in eternity, from eternity to eternity, He looked down upon us, and
He saw our tragedy, our predicament, our trouble, our sin and condemnation under the wrath of God. He saw it all, and He had compassion—that is the first thing.

Secondly, He did not think of Himself; He did not think of His rights. He did not say to Himself, 'I am the eternal Son of God, co-equal with the Father, co-eternal, sharing in all this splendour and absolute eternal glory.' 'He did not clutch at that,' said Paul—that is the meaning of He 'thought it not robbery to be equal.' He did not insist upon His rights; He did not think of Himself because He was so concerned about us. He thought of us; He was interested in our good. He was concerned about our being delivered and our being saved, and because of that He laid aside the insignia and the signs of His eternal glory. He placed that limitation upon Himself. He was born and laid in a manger as a baby; He was misunderstood; He worked as a carpenter—the One by whom the whole world was made making simple little things; and He endured the contradiction of sinners. 'Yet,' said Paul, 'He went on humbling Himself, down, down. He went even to the death and the shame of the cross. He was not thinking about Himself, nor about His rights and His pos-sessions. He thought of nothing but us and our need. He pitied our position, the hopelessness and the despair, so He laid down His life for us.'

That is the essence of love. It acts, it gives, it expresses itself; it cannot help itself—it *must*. May I suggest, in reverence, that it was because God is love that He created the world, something to love, in order to express this love because love must express itself. I may be wrong, I do not know, but it seems to me to be a necessity. True love is always active, and there we see it to perfection: God giving Himself for the evil, the perfect for the vile and the condemned.

'Let this mind be in you,' says the Apostle Paul (Phil 2:5). John puts it like this: 'Hereby we perceive the love of God, because he laid down his life for us: and we ought to lay down our lives for the brethren.' If the need should ever arise, there will be no hesitation if there is real love. If we love God, we will be ready to die for Him. The first Christians died by the thousands; they counted not their lives dear unto them, even unto death. They died for Him gladly, and they died for one another. If He did that for us and we say His love is in us, we shall do that for the brethren. And obviously if we are prepared to die for the brethren, we surely cannot refuse them when there is some little temporal, physical need. If we are called to the greater, surely the lesser, the smaller, the infinitesimal must be something that we do automatically.

'Herein we know love,' and this is how you get the whole of the doctrine of the Atonement in these few words: He laid down His life for us. Beloved friends, let us meditate upon these things; let us look at them; let us realise the nature of love and the implication of claiming that the love of God is in us. And then let us proceed to prove that we have it by loving one another, not in word, not in tongue, but in deed and in truth.

10

Condemnation, Confidence and Assurance

And hereby we know that we are of the truth, and shall assure our hearts before him. For if our heart condemn us, God is greater than our heart, and knoweth all things. Beloved, if our heart condemn us not, then have we confidence toward God. And whatsoever we ask, we receive of him, because we keep his commandments, and do those things that are pleasing in his sight. And this is his commandment, That we should believe on the name of his Son Jesus Christ, and love one another, as he gave us commandment.

1 JOHN 3:19–23

T he word 'hereby' at the beginning of the nineteenth verse reminds us that the Apostle is here continuing the subject, the theme, with which he has been dealing in the preceding verses; he has not finished with the subject yet. He presses the vital importance of really loving the brethren wholly, and he does it in this particular way in these verses that we are now considering.

First of all, he reminds us again that the subject under consideration–loving the brethren–is the proof that we are 'of the truth.'

'Hereby,' he says, 'we know that we are of the truth,' so that once
more we just hold on to that. It is a final proof of the fact that the
truth of God is really in us and is abiding in us. But, and this is his
main theme in this verse, this actual loving of the brethren is also,
he says, of tremendous importance in a very practical sense, and
that is from the standpoint of our own experience, and especially
our experience of communion with God in prayer. John now comes
right down and says something like this: 'If for no other reason, love
the brethren were it merely for your own sake, for the sake of your
own experience and especially for your experience in this matter of
prayer.'

Here again we are reminded of something that is always, it
seems to me, so plain in the Bible from beginning to end if we look
at it with a spiritual eye. There are certain laws in the spiritual life,
and they must be observed; sooner or later the truth will insist upon
having its place in us. Sooner or later, as the Bible puts it, our sins
will 'find us out,' however long we may go on apparently living a
kind of double life, subscribing intellectually to a body of doctrine
but failing in practise; sooner or later it will come home to us. We
cannot play fast and loose, according to John's argument here,
because a position will arise, and especially in this matter of prayer,
when we shall find ourselves denied perhaps the greatest thing of
all in our Christian experience.

That is the theme with which he deals in these verses–the place
of prayer in the life of the Christian in this world. Nothing is more
important than this in our worldly pilgrimage. Our Lord Himself
put that once and forever in a memorable verse. He said that 'Men
ought always to pray, and not to faint' (Luke 18:1); in other words,
if you do not pray, you will faint. The thing that keeps one going
in the Christian life is prayer–communion and fellowship with
God; it is something which is absolutely essential. I would go further and say that the Christian life is really impossible without it.
Read the Bible again with this in mind, and you will find that everywhere this is the thing that is emphasised. Look at the Psalms, for
instance. How often does the psalmist tell us that his friends had let
him down, his enemies were attacking him, and the people he had
relied upon most of all had forsaken him, but he thanks God that

the gate is still open. 'When my father and my mother forsake me, then the Lord will take me up' (Ps 27:10). As you listen to the men of God in their trouble, you hear that the one thing that keeps them going is their access to God in prayer. You find it in the Old Testament, and in the same way you see it in the New Testament. You see it in our Lord Himself; in the agony in the Garden of Gethsemane, He was praying to God, and Hebrews 5:7 is a comment on that. Read the biographies of God's people throughout the centuries, and you will find that this is something that stands out in an unmistakable manner. They were conscious of their dependence upon God, and they relied upon this access which they had to Him in prayer.

Now that is the matter with which John is dealing here, and his point is that we must be perfectly certain in our minds as to the conditions which control this whole question of prayer and access to God. So here he puts it in terms of this question of our loving the brethren, loving one another.

Let us take the matter in this way. The first question that John seems to raise is this: what is prayer? I wonder how often we stop to consider that, and yet it seems to me that it is a question which should always be uppermost in our minds. What exactly am I doing when I pray? Is it not our tendency to rush into prayer without considering what we are doing? Is it not our tendency to regard it as something automatic? Are we not always in danger of talking too easily about 'saying our prayers'?

There are many things which tend to encourage us to do that. Those who are more liturgical in their outlook have a habit of talking about 'saying a prayer,' and it seems to me that that is very different from the New Testament teaching on this whole subject. We do not 'say a prayer.' There is nothing automatic in it; indeed, I think a case should be made for saying that the most difficult thing of all is to pray. Prayer is not just a repetition of certain phrases, nor is it merely emitting certain desires or giving expression to certain beautiful thoughts. Prayer is not some process of auto-suggestion or of treating oneself by means of psychology, nor is it something that ought to make us feel better. It is not something, as I once remember hearing a man describe it, you do five minutes a day for your health's sake, so that you always feel better when you utter these beautiful thoughts. That is not the New Testament idea of prayer, nor that of the Old Testament.

What is prayer? Well, I cannot think of a better way of describing it than these two words which we have at the end of verse 19: 'Hereby we know that we are of the truth, and shall assure our hearts *before him.*' That is prayer; prayer is coming before Him. Now, we are always in the presence of God–'in him we live, and move, and have our being' (Acts 17:28)–and we are always under His eye. But prayer is something still more special. Prayer is having a special audience and going immediately and directly to Him–'before him.' Prayer is something in which we turn our backs upon everything else, excluding everything else, while, for the time being, we find ourselves face to face with God alone. There is a sense in which one cannot expound it further; it is just that.

The first thing, then, that we have to realise always in this matter of prayer is that that is exactly and precisely what we do when we pray. Obviously, therefore, in a sense the most vital thing in prayer is just that realisation that we are before Him. And you will find that the saints have always talked a great deal about this. That is the difficulty; thoughts will keep on obtruding themselves, and our imaginations will wander all over the world, and certain ideas and proposals and wants and needs will intrude, but all that must be dismissed, and we must just start by realising that we are actually and literally in the presence of the living God. 'Before him'!

Now, says John, this whole question of brotherly love is of importance because of that. It is when you come there, when you are before Him, that you begin to realise the importance of what you are doing with the rest of your life and with the rest of your time. It is when you come there that you begin to see the relevance of this.

That is the very essence of prayer, so that always and at all times, whether alone or together in the house of God, that is the thing that should be uppermost and predominant. I think we would say less at times if we realised that. There would certainly be no room whatever for any cleverness or mere effort to try to utter beautiful thoughts and phrases; we would not be concerned about things like that. Realising His presence, we would be lost to all such things; we would be intent upon this communion and this fellowship with Him.

That, then, is the general idea, but let us come right down to the particular as John here expounds it. If that is what is meant by prayer, what are the conditions of true prayer, or what is essential to it? The matters that John expounds here are of vital importance. The first thing that is absolutely vital and essential to true prayer is freedom from a sense of condemnation. 'Hereby we know that we are of the truth, and shall assure our hearts'—or reassure, or persuade, our hearts—'before him. For if our heart condemn us . . .'— that is it! If your heart is condemning you, or if your heart is against you, there will be no true prayer. The first thing that is essential is a deliverance, a freedom, from a sense of condemnation.

I suppose there is nothing which really tests us so much as being in the position or the attitude of prayer. It is when we are truly praying before Him that we actually realise what we are. This is a much more thorough test than a talk or a discussion. We can be tested by talking to people about spiritual things, or as we discuss them together; even preaching an address or a sermon should be a means of testing. It is meant that all these things should test us, but I suggest they do not test us in the same way that prayer does. I suggest that prayer is a more thorough test also than thought or meditation. These too should test us, and we should spend time in thinking and meditating. Indeed, we go on to self-examination, but I say that prayer tests us in a way that even self-examination does not test us. Self-examination can be a very painful process as we look at the New Testament description of the Christian and examine ourselves in the light of this Word. But, I suggest, nothing makes us so see ourselves as we are as being there in prayer before Him.

This is so for this reason, that when we are in this attitude of prayer, we are no longer in control. The very fact that I get on my knees in prayer (and that is the value of kneeling), that very fact in and of itself is a submission. I am there submitting myself, I am abandoning myself. Now while I am talking, I am in control, and while I am discussing I am in control. Someone may be examining me, but I am still able to defend myself. When I am engaged in thought and meditation, I am still in control. But when I get on my knees in prayer, then, in a sense, I am doing nothing, I am submitting myself, I am abandoning myself before Him. It is He who is in control, it is He who is doing everything, and that is why prayer tests us in a way which nothing else can possibly do.

Now this is not theory. I am sure I am speaking to the experience of many. Is this not what happens when you truly pray? I do not mean when you repeat the Lord's Prayer or some mechanical prayer you have made for yourself. Nor do I mean when you rush and offer a number of petitions when you need something very desperately. I mean when you shut the door and are alone in your room, or wherever it is, and you kneel down and you realise that you are before Him.

Is this not what happens? Something within you begins to speak; it is what John here calls the 'heart.' It is the conscience, but it is something more than the conscience. The conscience begins to act and to speak, and this is what happens: We remember certain things we have done and said. We had forgotten them, we would never have reminded ourselves of them, but back they come. The angry expression, the unworthy thought, the unkind deed—as you are there alone with God, these things—the things you failed to do, the broken vows and pledges and so on—come back, and they condemn. We remember how when, perhaps, the last time we were like that alone with God we protested our love and we promised Him we would go out to serve Him, but we have not. We have forgotten our promise, and a voice within us says, 'You are a cad; you have no right to pray to God. Who are you to come into the presence of God?' We are made conscious of our utter unworthiness and our failure and our smallness and our foulness; our hearts condemn us. They bring up all these things against us, and there they say, 'Look at yourself—compare yourself to the saints—what right have you to ask God anything—what right have you to submit your petitions to God?' Do we not know about this?

But that is not all. There is something further, and that brings me to the twentieth verse: 'For if our heart condemn us, God is greater than our heart, and knoweth all things.' Now I suppose that there has been more controversy over the exact meaning of this verse than over many verses in the Bible. I am seriously tempted to give you a list of the great commentators of the centuries and to show you how they have taken different sides with regard to the interpretation of this verse; all equally good Christians, and yet they have taken different views. There are two main views which have been advocated. One view says that this is a great verse of comfort, and that what John is really saying is that if, there in the presence of God—before Him—your heart does condemn you, do not be downcast. It is all right, for God is greater than our heart. He knows our desires in spite of our failure in practise; all things are open unto Him; He knows everything, and with Him there is mercy and grace and compassion. Though your heart condemns you, God beholds and forgives you; be confident in your prayer. That is one view.

The other view is the exact opposite. 'If our heart condemn us,' if my own heart makes me feel and know I am a sinner and that I am a cad, if my own heart does that, how much more shall God, for God is greater than my heart and 'knoweth all things.' I do not know everything about myself; at that point there before Him, I know enough. Alas, I know more than I like to know, and I know that even then I do not know half the truth about myself and my sinful nature. There are secret faults of which I am unaware. God sees me in a way I do not see myself; He sees into the innermost recesses. If my heart condemns me, what must be my position in the sight of God?

Now I am not going to give a list of the great names, but let it suffice to say that two great Reformers took different sides; Luther took one side and John Calvin the other, and other men have been divided through the centuries. Bengel agreed with Luther, and Charles Simeon agreed with Calvin; so the division has been manifested from the beginning. Obviously, then, we cannot hope to decide this matter conclusively, and it seems to me that we must all decide this for ourselves, but for myself I cannot but take the view that this verse is not meant to comfort us, and my reasons for that will be given in the paragraphs to follow.

It seems to me that to interpret this verse as one of comfort is to contradict the whole purpose of the passage, which is to warn us, to exhort us. Read the whole passage on brotherly love again, and you will find that its whole purpose is to search us and to make us examine ourselves and to warn us against assuming glibly that all is well when it is not. It is to warn; and not only that, it seems to me that if we regard this as comfort, we are doing something which is very dangerous. We are silencing the voice of conscience and of the heart by talking about 'the love of God.' We are all very ready to do that; we are all very ready to avoid the point of conviction by saying, 'God loves me, and all is well.' To me that is a dangerous thing to do. Indeed, does it not lead directly to antinomianism? Is not the argument for antinomianism just that? The love of God covers me; therefore I can do anything I like. I say I am forgiven and all is well and I become slack about my conduct. To me that is surely the height of danger, and I argue that the ultimate proof is to be found again in the beginning of the nineteenth verse: 'Hereby we know that we are of the truth.' That is John's argument, which is a reference to what he has been saying. The way I am to reassure my heart when it does condemn me is not to say, 'God knows everything, and God therefore loves me.' No, it is something that I myself have been doing—'hereby,' by loving my brethren in deed and in truth and not merely in word and in thought. If you do that, says John, you will be able to reassure your heart.

So I put the argument like this: Here we are on our knees in prayer; we are 'before him,' and we are conscious of the presence of God. Our lives are being searched and examined as by some invisible searchlight, some X-ray; the eye of God is upon us, all these things are brought to the surface, and our hearts are condemning us. Well, while we are in that state we cannot pray, we are condemned; we do not know what to do with ourselves. Now we have to talk to ourselves; we must reassure these hearts of ours; we must persuade them that we have this access and that all is well.

So how do we do it? 'You do it like this,' says John; 'your heart is there reminding you of all these things, condemning you. You say to your heart, "It is all right; I admit that all that is absolutely true of me, and I bemoan and regret it. Yes, but I do find that I love the brethren. I find myself drawn out to them. I love their society and their company; I cannot look and see my brother or sister suffer without helping them. I find myself loving them, thus, in practise, and because I do that, I must be a child of God—I would not do it otherwise. The fact that I am thus loving the brethren is a proof that I have passed from death unto life. It means that I no longer belong to the world; it means I am a child of God. By nature I would not love such people, I would not be interested in them, I would not be concerned to help them, but I find the desire in me to do so and I am doing it; and though what you say against me is true, I say that this is a proof that I am a child of God. So I can reassure my heart, and that is why I do it.'" Have you not known yourself having to do that kind of thing? Have you not known this argument with yourself there in the presence of God, and have you not had to find this confidence in terms of Scripture and to prove to yourself that you are a child of God and therefore can pray to Him?

The interesting point to me here is that John puts the argument in that particular way. Why does he not tell us, I wonder, that the way to reassure our hearts before Him is to think of the Cross and to remind ourselves of the death of our Lord for us? Now here, I think, we see the very depth and profundity of John's teaching. You see, he is concerned about people who are much too ready to fly to the Cross. John knows that the human heart is desperately wicked, and he knows the danger of men and women referring everything to the Cross, in order that they may have ease and peace of mind and conscience and then go on with their sin. We find the same thing exactly in Hebrews chapter 10, but this test of John's—I say it with reverence—is even stronger than the other. I have known a drunken man tell me that he is relying upon the Cross; I have known people speak of the Cross with tears and then continue in their drunken, unworthy life. There is a terrible danger here; men and women may make intellectual assent to truth and then fail, but John's test makes that impossible.

If I am truly loving the brethren, that is not something intellectual; people who really do love and prove it in practise are not those who are merely giving intellectual assent; their lives are proof of the fact that they are born again. And if they are born again, they must be forgiven, and the Cross is covering them. John puts a more thoroughgoing test, the test not only of experience but of experience

proving itself in practise–'Hereby we know that we are of the truth
because we love the brethren.' That is the first thing–we must be
utterly and entirely free from a sense of condemnation.

Let me say a word on the second condition, which is *confidence*
(v 21): 'Beloved, if our heart condemn us not, then have we confidence toward God.' Now that first stage of which we have been
speaking is not enough in and of itself. It is negative because, as I
have emphasised, we have to get rid of the sense of condemnation,
because while we are unhappy about ourselves and our whole position we cannot pray with confidence; the sense of condemnation
holds us down, and we cannot bring our petitions and our requests
to God.

Again I put that to you in terms of your own experience. Have
you not known what it is to have an experience like this? You suddenly find yourself in a crisis–perhaps you are ill, perhaps someone dear to you is ill, or you may be confronted by some critical
position owing to something that has happened to you, and you are
at the end of your tether. So you say, 'I will pray to God,' and you
get on your knees, and the moment you do so comes this thought:
'But you have no right to pray; you are a cad, you have forgotten
God, you only turn to God when you are in trouble.' So you somehow have no confidence in your prayer; you are uncertain. 'Now,'
says John, 'you cannot pray truly and you cannot have fellowship
unless you have confidence.' So you settle that first thing; you must
get rid of the sense of condemnation, but then, having done that,
you go on to this second step.

Now this matter of confidence is absolutely vital to true prevailing prayer. Let me remind you how the Scripture puts it. Have
you noticed that word 'boldness' that is used in connection with
prayer in the Scriptures? You often find it in the epistle to the
Hebrews: 'Let us come boldly unto the throne of grace, that we
may obtain mercy, and find grace to help in time of need' (Heb
4:16), or again, 'Having therefore, brethren, boldness to enter into
the holiest by the blood of Jesus' (Heb 10:19), or, 'let us draw near
with a true heart in full assurance of faith' (Heb 10:22). Or consider
what Paul says in Ephesians 3: 'In whom we have boldness and
access with confidence by the faith of him' (v 12). That is the way

to pray; if our petitions are to be of any value, we must have boldness and assurance and confidence in our access.

How is this to be obtained? Well, it seems to me that we are
here dealing with the answer, and it is still this question of sonship.
The consciousness of our sonship and the assurance of our sonship
is again something to be determined by our love of the brethren. It
works like this: if I am truly loving the brethren, then I remember
that I am a child of God. Therefore, when I am before God in
prayer I argue like this: I must think of God now not as my Judge
but as my Father. John goes on to remind us of that in the next
chapter. I do not come to God, therefore, in a spirit of fear, because
'fear hath torment' (4:18). But I go rather in the spirit of love, and
'perfect love casteth out fear' (4:18). So, assured of my sonship, I
know that God delights in me, that God indeed is much more ready
to bless me than I am to ask to be blessed. I know He is ready and
willing and waiting to grant me everything that is for my good;
assured of my sonship, I know that 'all things work together for
good to them that love God, to them who are the called according
to his purpose' (Rom 8:28). In other words, the only thing that
really can give me confidence in prayer before God is this utter,
absolute assurance that I am a child of God, and I go as a child to
my Father–that is the basis of confidence. So you see the same thing
gives me confidence as has already, negatively, delivered me from
a sense of condemnation.

But that brings me to the third and last condition, and that is
what we must call *assurance*. 'Beloved, if our heart condemn us not,
then have we confidence toward God. And whatsoever we ask, we
receive of him, because we keep his commandments, and do those
things that are pleasing in his sight.' He has already put it in terms
of assuring our hearts before Him. Now this is the final statement.
Over and above my confidence is my right of access; I must have
assurance with regard to my petitions.

James puts it like this: 'If any of you lack wisdom, let him ask
of God . . .' But notice this: 'But let him ask in faith, nothing waver-
ing: for he that wavereth is like a wave of the sea driven with the
wind and tossed. For let not that man think that he shall receive any
thing of the Lord' (Jas 1:5-7). If you are uncertain, doubtful or hes-

itant and lacking assurance in your petition, you will not get your request, says James. Listen to the psalmist in Psalm 66:18: 'If I regard iniquity in my heart, the Lord will not hear me.' If I go to God with a double mind, holding on to my sin and knowing that I am living a wrong life, I will have no confidence in my prayer. 'God is greater than my heart and knoweth all things'; yes, if I am condemning myself and know I am wrong, how much more so must God.

Now I think that our Lord Himself has answered this question in certain teaching which you will find recorded in the Gospel according to St. John. He put it like this: 'If ye abide in me, and my words abide in you, ye shall ask what ye will, and it shall be done unto you' (John 15:7). Or again: 'I have chosen you, and ordained you, that ye should go forth and bear fruit, and that your fruit should remain; that whatsoever ye shall ask of the Father in my name, he may give it you' (John 15:16). Now John puts that like this: 'Whatsoever we ask, we receive of Him, because we go on keeping His commandments and we go on doing those things that are pleasing in His sight.'

'Does he mean,' asks someone, 'that as long as I live a good life, anything I may ask God in prayer I am certain and guaranteed to receive?' Oh, no! What it means is this: if I am keeping His commandments, if I am really doing His will, if I love God and my neighbour as myself, if I really am living the Christian life in that way, then I can be certain that my life is a life which is being controlled by the Holy Spirit, and therefore I know that any petitions and desires I may have, have been created within me by the Holy Spirit. And because my petitions and my desires are produced by the Holy Spirit, I can be certain that they will be answered. 'We know not what we should pray for as we ought: but the Spirit itself maketh intercession for us with groanings which cannot be uttered' (Rom 8:26). We do not always understand what we are saying, but 'He that searcheth the hearts knoweth what is the mind of the Spirit, because he maketh intercession for the saints according to the will of God' (Rom 8:27)—that is it.

In other words, if I live the life, keeping the commandments and loving my brethren, that is proof that I am being controlled by the Holy Spirit, and in that state the Holy Spirit is dictating my prayer to me, and that prayer will be answered. But if I am not living the life, then my petitions are probably arising from the flesh, from my own carnal nature, and I must not be surprised and disappointed if my requests are not answered and granted to me.

We see prayer perfectly again in the case of the Lord Jesus Christ Himself. Look at Him. He obeyed God's commandments perfectly, and He received the Holy Spirit without measure. He was led and guided of the Spirit. He had put aside His own eternal glory, and He came to live as man. Then He received the Spirit and was guided and led by the Spirit and thus He lived this life of prayer. Remember how He prayed, 'Father, if thou be willing, remove this cup from me: nevertheless, not my will, but thine, be done' (Luke 22:42).

His supreme object and desire was to do the will of His Father, and as long as that is our supreme will and desire, as long as we are concerned about that and are submitting to the leading of the Spirit, our requests will be granted as His requests were granted. God answered Him and granted His requests, and the nearer we approximate to Him, in the same way we can be certain that our requests will be granted. 'Whatsoever we ask, we receive of him, because we keep his commandments, and do those things that are pleasing in his sight. And this is his commandment, that we should believe on the name of his Son Jesus Christ, and love one another, as he gave us commandment' (v 23).

So there you are 'before him.' Have you confidence in your prayer? Do your prayers avail; have you assurance about them? These are the things that are necessary; you reassure your heart, you get rid of condemnation, you are confident as a child of God, and above it all you have the assurance which is given alone by the Holy Spirit, by His indwelling within you and by His life in your life and in your very petitions. What a glorious, wondrous thing this is—we come before Him, we have audience with the King, we speak to the living God.

11

The Holy Spirit

And he that keepeth his commandments dwelleth in him,
and he in him. And hereby we know that he abideth in us,
by the Spirit which he hath given us.

1 JOHN 3:24

In this verse we have the first specific and explicit mention of the
Holy Spirit in this particular passage. We have had in the second chapter an indirect reference to Him, where the Apostle has
reminded us of the unction which we have from the Holy One and
the anointing which we have received of Him. But here is the actual
expression, the Spirit with a capital *S*. It is not a reference to some
vague spirit that is in man, in the sense in which we often use the
word when we speak of man's nature or temperament or character. It is a reference to the gift of the Holy Spirit, and here John is
introducing a further proof of our sonship. The theme which has
been occupying him right through this third chapter has been that
we are the children of God. That, he says, is one of the most vital
things which we can ever grasp in this life and in this world.

Now John, you remember, is writing to Christian people in the
first century who were having a very difficult time, knowing persecution and suffering and misunderstanding. The world then was
remarkably like the world today, and John sums it all up in this
phrase: 'We know that we are of God, and the whole world lieth in
wickedness' (5:19). That is his object—to help, to comfort and to

encourage these Christian people who were living their Christian lives in such a difficult and gainsaying world. There are certain things, he says, which they must hold in their minds. The first is that they are in fellowship with God and are walking with Him. Then the second great theme is that of sonship, that we are the children of God. The Christian is nothing less than that—you cannot be a Christian without being a child of God. John holds up this glorious concept, you remember, in those three noble verses at the beginning of this chapter, with their almost incomparable statement of the Christian position.

But John, with his practical pastoral mind and intent, was most concerned that these people should show it. It is no use talking about being children of God unless we really are giving practical proof of that fact now. Unless we give that practical proof, we will not have the assurance—that is his theme. And let me remind you, he says, that there are certain things that we must never lose sight of in that connection. The first is, we must keep the commandments: 'He that doeth righteousness is righteous, even as he is righteous' (3:7). Then he comes on to the second great proof of our sonship—that is, our love for one another, love of the brethren: 'We know that we have passed from death unto life, because we love the brethren' (v 14).

And now here he tells us that there is still an additional proof of our sonship, and that is the reception of the Holy Spirit: 'Hereby we know that he abideth in us.' If we are children, it means that He is in us and we are in Him; and if you want proof of that fact, says John, here it is—'by the Spirit which he hath given us.' So, we are face to face with this great doctrine and truth concerning the Holy Spirit. It is to be found everywhere in the New Testament, and it is absolutely vital and essential to the true Christian position and to Christian experience. And here, in this one verse, John presents the doctrine to us in what seems to me to be a most interesting manner. He combines what we may call the objective and the subjective in one verse. He reminds us of the great fact, and yet he reminds us at the same time of the complement of the fact in personal experience.

It is to this that I am anxious to call your attention now, and I think that the best division of our subject is this: First of all we must consider the gift or the place of the Holy Spirit in the plan of salvation, and we look at that in this way: First, we must look at the fact, about which we can read in Acts 2. We are confronted there with a fact of which we must never lose sight. That is history, and if we do not realise that it is history, quite as much as the various other facts that are recorded in the Bible, then our whole position is wrong.

There in Jerusalem on that Day of Pentecost so long ago, this astounding and amazing thing happened. There that group of people met together in the upper room, and suddenly this tremendous thing happened. The Holy Ghost descended upon them as 'cloven tongues like as of fire' (Acts 2:3); the whole place was shaken, and these people were transformed. This wonderful thing happened to them, and they began to speak; they had the gift of speaking in other languages, so that the people, who had come together at Jerusalem for the feast of Pentecost from the various parts of the then inhabited and civilised world, all heard these men speaking in their own languages and telling about the wonderful works of God. That is just literal, actual history, and this day on which I am preaching to you[1] does insist upon our emphasising that fact. Of course, we do have to deal with it subjectively, but the big thing we must start with is this objective fact, this historical event that there in Jerusalem, literally and actually, the Holy Ghost came down upon the early church—the gift was given.

Now many authorities believe that this verse is a reference to that and that only, that it is a direct pointer to the Day of Pentecost at Jerusalem. Well, to say the very least, that is included, and that must always come first. We realise that from that moment onwards the Christian Church was constituted in a new sense and began to function as the Christian Church in a way which it had never done before, and we realise too that we today are just a continuation of that which began there so long ago. It is, I say, a fact—a mighty fact, one of the great turning points of history, one of the most significant events in the whole story of the human race.

That, then, is the fact, but let us also consider something of the meaning of this fact. We are still discussing the place of the Holy

Spirit in the plan of salvation. What was the significance and the meaning of that which happened there on the Day of Pentecost? Here are some of the things.

That was the last step in the series of great acts or enactments in connection with the plan of salvation. Now, the glory of our position as Christians is that we do not so much believe a teaching as that we believe truths which result from events and happenings. Christianity is not a philosophy; it includes philosophy, but it is not just that. You are not a Christian in the sense that you may be a Platonist or an Aristotelian. It must not be thought of like that. We are saved not by believing a truth; we are saved because of what God has done for us.

Therefore this event on the Day of Pentecost at Jerusalem is an event that you must put into a certain series. You start way back in the Garden of Eden when man fell and when God spoke and gave a promise. Then you come on to all the history that is recorded in the Old Testament. The Flood, the call of Abraham, the isolation of that man and the turning of him into a nation—that is all God doing something, it is God acting. Then you go on right through the Old Testament history; the going down into Egypt, the going out of Egypt, the crossing of the Red Sea—all these are events, part of the great plan of salvation.

And when you turn to the New Testament, there are crucial facts which we must always hold on to. Consider the birth of Jesus Christ in Bethlehem—that fact is absolutely essential. He, the Son of God, was there born as a babe and placed in a manger; this is the Incarnation, that shattering, cataclysmic event when God came on earth in the form and in the likeness of human flesh. Then you go on and you see certain other crucial facts and events. They are all of vital importance, but some we obviously must single out.

You come especially to the Crucifixion. There is something which is basic to our salvation. In other words, as Christians we do not just speak about the love of God which forgives us. We say God's love forgives us because He did something there on the cross of Calvary. Without Calvary there is no forgiveness—an event, a fact, that which took place literally upon that hill, upon that tree—the Crucifixion. Then the next great fact is the Resurrection. He rose from the grave—He could not be held by it, and He literally came out of that tomb on the morning of the third day; it is a fact, it is history. Then the Ascension; He actually rose from amongst those disciples and went into Heaven. Again it is an event, a fact. And here, at Pentecost, we have what we may well call the last great step in the series of acts or enactments or events which made our salvation possible.

That is the way in which we must understand what happened there at Jerusalem on that day. It was God again doing something; it was an event; it was essential to our receiving this great salvation. That is the series into which it must go and to which it belongs.

The second thing is that the sending of the Holy Ghost thus upon the early church on the Day of Pentecost is the final proof of our Lord's claim for Himself. It is this because it proves that Jesus of Nazareth is in reality the only begotten Son of God. That was Peter's argument in the sermon which he preached to the people on that day; that is what he set out to prove. He said, 'You crucified Jesus of Nazareth. You did not realise who He was; you felt Him to be an imposter and a blasphemer, and that is why you put Him away. But there are certain things which prove that He is what He claimed to be, the Son of God. The Resurrection proved it. But,' says Peter, 'here is something further. You have looked at me and at my brethren and you have said, "These men are drunk and full of new wine. They are talking in languages we can understand, and they seem to be possessed." No, no,' says Peter, 'I will tell you what this is. This means that Jesus, whom you rejected, is, as He claimed to be, the Son of God. And when He died and arose from the grave and ascended into Heaven, God, according to His ancient promise, gave Him the gift of the Holy Ghost to give to His people; and He has given that gift, and that is what has happened to us. God has fulfilled His promise; He has given to Him the gift of the Holy Spirit, and He, Christ, has sent the Holy Spirit. And that proves that He must be the Son of God, the Christ, the Saviour of the world.'

So this event, this fact, is of crucial importance in this whole matter of salvation. That is—let me emphasise this again—the final, ultimate proof of the unique Deity and Sonship of the Lord Jesus Christ. It is there we have this final statement of the fact that He is

the Son of the eternal Father. The Father gives Him the gift, and
He passes it on to us; so the gift comes from the Father and the Son.

But let us also look at it like this: The gift of the Holy Ghost to
the Church is also, then, the absolute proof of the sufficiency of the
work of Christ and of its acceptance with God. The crucial question in a sense is whether that work of Christ on the cross is indeed
sufficient. The problem is, how can God forgive sinful men? How
can this Holy God conceivably or possibly forgive sin? The answer
is, the death of Jesus Christ upon the cross; but is that sufficient?
How can we know that God has accepted that work? How do we
know that God has accepted the offer of Christ when He went into
heaven and offered Himself and His own blood and said, 'Here is
the sacrifice that I offer for sin'? What proof have we of the acceptance of it?

Again the Resurrection is partly the answer, but the New
Testament constantly tells us that, in a sense, the ultimate proof of
that action is the coming and the sending of the Holy Spirit, for that
means that God the Father said to the Son, 'I accept your work, it
is sufficient; You have died for the redeemed, they are Your people.
So I will give you My Spirit to give to them, and then they will
know that they are Your people and My people. I forgive them
freely, and here I will give proof of it.' Therefore, the event that took
place on the Day of Pentecost at Jerusalem is of tremendous and
vital importance in giving us this assurance of the acceptance and
the sufficiency of the work of Jesus Christ for us.

I can put it still further like this: The coming of the Holy Spirit
is the means whereby salvation is mediated to us. Do you remember what our Lord said to His disciples just before His death? They
were crestfallen and unhappy as He was talking to them increasingly of His departure and about His going away. He said to them,
'It is expedient for you that I go away'—it is a good thing, it is ben-
eficial to you that I go away—'for if I go not away, the Comforter
will not come unto you; but if I depart, I will send him unto you'
(John 16:7).

Now that means this, and I say it with reverence—do we always
realise, Christian people, that you and I who have never seen the
Lord Jesus Christ with the eye of flesh are in a much more advan-

tageous position than were His own disciples who looked into His face? Are we not often guilty, in our folly and misunderstanding of the Scriptures, of saying, 'Oh, if only I had been alive when He was here, if only I could have seen Him with my eyes, then I would have believed in a way that I do not now.' But that is utterly unscriptural. He said, 'It is expedient for you that I go away'—by which he meant that it is only because He has gone away, because He has done His work and has sent the Holy Spirit to dwell within us, that the result of His work really becomes part of our life and experience. It is through the work of the Holy Spirit that the perfect, finished work of Christ upon the cross and His mediation is transmitted to us and enters our lives; so it means that.

And then the last thing I would say about it in this connection is that, of course, the sending of the Holy Spirit upon the Church on the Day of Pentecost was the ultimate fulfilment of the promise of God. Can you not hear the thrill in the voice of Peter as he speaks those words: 'This is that which was spoken by the prophet Joel'? It is one of God's ancient promises, one of the most glorious of all. God has said that He is going to pour out His Spirit; the young men shall dream dreams, and even the unenlightened will understand truth. It will no longer be only a certain few, select people who will know the truth. The common people shall understand. 'I will pour out my Spirit,' and the great salvation will come to all and sundry. And here God has fulfilled the old promises; He has sent and has given the gift of the Holy Spirit.

We have, then, looked briefly at the gift of the Holy Spirit in the plan of salvation. That is its place, and that is the real way to look at it, so that as Christian people we must never be guilty of stopping either at Calvary or at the Resurrection. I put it like that because I often fear that we do that. We give a place to the cross, and to the Resurrection, but we do not always come to the Day of Pentecost, and that shows that we have not known the relevance of this. This is the ultimate step, the last step in the great series and one which is essential and vital to our salvation.

So, having looked at it objectively, let us become a little more subjective. My second principle is that the Christian is one who has received the gift of the Holy Ghost. 'Hereby we know that he abideth in us, by the Spirit which he hath given us.' What is a Christian? I am never tired of putting forward that question, because I think that of all the things that are misunderstood in the world today this is the one that is most misunderstood. What is a Christian–a good person, a moral person, a formal member of a church, one who pays an occasional visit to God's house? Is that a Christian? Shame upon us if ever we have given that impression! No, a Christian is pneumatic, spiritual. Is that not the statement of the New Testament everywhere–a *spiritual* man or woman?

A spiritual person is one who has received the Holy Spirit–that is New Testament terminology. Christians are people who are altogether different from those who are not Christians. They are not just a little bit better, or people who do certain things. No, they themselves are different; they are spiritual. 'We have received,' says Paul, 'not the spirit of the world, but the Spirit which is of God; that we may know the things that are freely given to us of God. . . . He that is spiritual judgeth all things' (1 Cor 2:12, 15); but not the natural man–that is the difference, naturally and spiritually.

Now, there are some people who say that you become a Christian and then later you receive the gift of the Holy Spirit. But you cannot be a Christian unless you have received the gift of the Holy Spirit. It is that, in a sense, that makes you a Christian. It means this new birth; it means being born again; it means, to use the language of Peter, to be 'partakers of the divine nature' (2 Pet 1:4). It means, to use the language of our blessed Lord Himself, that God is *abiding* in us. 'He that keepeth his commandments,' says John, 'dwelleth in him, and he in him.' And if you want the best commentary on that, read for yourselves John 14, those great words of our Lord: 'I will not leave you comfortless: I will come to you' (v 18); or, as some would translate it, 'I will not leave you orphans, I will come again.' 'I will come through the gift of the Holy Spirit; I will send another Comforter, and the result of His coming will be that He will dwell in you–I and the Father will dwell in you.'

These are the amazing words describing the mystical union of the believer and Christ and God, and here it all is in a phrase in 1 John 3. Surely if all of us who claim the name of Christian only realised that and what it means to be a Christian, not only would the whole church on earth be transformed, but I think the world would be shaken. If we but realised that this is the Christian, the spiritual man or woman with the Holy Spirit, with God dwelling in us, if we but realised that, I think our world would rather look at us and say, 'What is the matter with these people—what is this?' And we would be able to give the same answer as Peter gave way back so long ago in Jerusalem: 'This is that which was spoken by the prophet Joel.' We have received the Holy Spirit, and we are therefore what we are. That is the Christian.

Let me come to my last principle. How may we know that we have the Spirit? That is obviously the vital question. That is the basis of my assurance; that is how I know that He dwells in me; that is the practical question. How do we know that the Holy Spirit has come to us, that we have received the gift of the Holy Ghost? I shall simply suggest a number of headings by way of an answer.

Here are the things that are taught by the New Testament. Those who have received the Holy Spirit are aware of a power dealing with them and working in them. 'Work out your own salvation with fear and trembling: for it is God which worketh in you both to will and to do of his good pleasure' (Phil 2:12-13). A disturbance, something, someone interfering in our lives. We are going along, and suddenly we are arrested and pulled up, and we find ourselves different. That is the beginning; that is what always happens when the Holy Ghost begins to work in a human being. There is a disturbance, an interruption to the normal ordinary tenor of life. There is something different, an awareness of being dealt with—I cannot put it better; that is the essence of the Holy Spirit dealing with us.

Then it leads to this, that we find ourselves beginning to take an interest in these things, in a spiritual sense. Paul says that they who are carnal 'mind the things of the flesh,' but the Christian, he says, is the one who minds 'the things of the Spirit' (Rom 8:5)—he is interested in them. Non-Christians say that the Bible is a terribly boring book, and when you talk about spiritual things, they do not know what you are talking about. I am not criticising them; I rather pity them. They just do not understand, and the whole thing is boring and has no relevance to life.

If you feel like that about these things, you have not received the Spirit, because when people receive the Spirit, they find themselves curiously interested in these things. They are amazed at the fact that they could ever have lived without them. This, they say, is the most wonderful thing of all. They are no longer interested in the mechanics of religion. You can be interested in that, in the work of the church or in your work in the church, without being interested in the Spirit. That is not what I am talking about; those who have received the Spirit are spiritually interested in truth.

And that leads to the next thing, which is the conviction of sin. They are men and women who see themselves unworthy and guilty before God. They begin to see that their nature is wrong, and they hate it. That is the Spirit—He leads them to believe on the Lord Jesus Christ and to understand the truth. John has already told us: 'This is the commandment, that we should believe on the name of his Son Jesus Christ' (v 23). Only the Holy Spirit can enable us to see Jesus Christ as the Son of God and the Saviour of our souls. You will dismiss Him entirely until the Spirit enlightens you; but once He works, you begin to see and understand the truth. Then you are aware of a new life within you; you are conscious of a new being, and a new nature. 'I live; yet not I, but Christ liveth in me' (Gal 2:20). I cannot understand myself; there is 'the old man' still—the man that I do understand, but there is someone else, because I have become a new creature.

And then there are the fruits of the Spirit. The fruit of the Spirit is love, joy, peace, love of the brethren. Once the Spirit comes in, the fruits of the Spirit begin to show themselves—hatred of sin, desires for holiness. We love God's commandments, as John says in chapter 5: 'His commandments are not grievous.' Christians begin to love them, and they want to show the fruit of the Spirit in that way.

This is that 'Spirit of adoption, whereby we cry, Abba, Father' (Rom 8:15), and we know what the Scripture means when it says, 'the Spirit itself beareth witness with our spirit, that we are the children of God' (Rom 8:16). Those are some of the things that you recognise. It means holiness is in you. Do you recognise all of these things? These are the proofs of the indwelling of the Holy Spirit.

There were also those gifts which God gave on the Day of Pentecost; they may still be given. Yes, I may, in His sovereign will, still get these. The gifts of the Spirit also are a proof of the indwelling of the Spirit.

Take, then, all those things together and there are the proofs of the fact that we have received the Holy Ghost. Oh, the marvel and the wonder of such a gift, the free gift. In spite of our sin and shame, in spite of our unworthiness and all that is so true of us, this amazing God has given us His own Spirit, and with the Spirit He comes to dwell and to abide in us. What a wondrous gift! What an amazing gift that God, the eternal, should come and dwell in us and enable us to dwell in Him. 'Hereby we know that he abideth in us, by the Spirit which he hath given us.'

NOTES

CHAPTER ONE: Children of God
1. Cf. the earlier Vols. 1, 2 in this series, *Fellowship with God* and *Walking with God* (Crossway Books, 1992, 1993).

CHAPTER THREE: Holiness
1. This sermon was preached in the season of Lent, on 3rd April, 1949.
2. Cf. *Fellowship with God*, Vol. 1 of this series (Crossway Books, 1992).

CHAPTER FOUR: The Sinless Saviour
1. Cf. *Fellowship with God*, Vol. 1 of this series (Crossway Books, 1992).
2. This sermon was preached on Palm Sunday, 1949.
3. See *Walking with God*, Vol. 2 of this series (Crossway Books, 1993).
4. "There Is a Green Hill Far Away," by Cecil Frances Alexander.

CHAPTER FIVE: Victory over the Devil
1. This sermon was preached on Easter Sunday, 1949.

CHAPTER EIGHT: The Marks of a Christian
1. Readers will be glad to know that the wife herself became a Christian soon afterwards. *Ed.*

CHAPTER ELEVEN: The Holy Spirit
1. This sermon was preached on Whit Sunday, 1949.